PRAISE FOR *DEBATING AMERICAN HISTORY*

"*Debating American History* repositions the discipline of history as one that is rooted in discovery, investigation, and interpretation."
—Ingrid Dineen-Wimberly,
University of California, Santa Barbara

"*Debating American History* is an excellent replacement for a 'big assignment' in a course. Offering a way to add discussion to a class, it is also a perfect 'active learning' assignment, in a convenient package."
—Gene Rhea Tucker, Temple College

"The advantage that *Debating American History* has over other projects and texts currently available is that it brings a very clear and focused organization to the notion of classroom debate. The terms of each debate are clear. The books introduce students to historiography and primary sources. Most of all, the project re-envisions the way that US history should be taught. No other textbook or set of teaching materials does what these books do when taken together as the sum of their parts."
—Ian Hartman, University of Alaska

DEBATING AMERICAN HISTORY

THE CAUSES OF THE CIVIL WAR

DEBATING AMERICAN HISTORY

Series Editors: Joel M. Sipress, David J. Voelker

DEBATING AMERICAN HISTORY

THE CAUSES OF THE CIVIL WAR

Joel M. Sipress

UNIVERSITY OF WISCONSIN–SUPERIOR

NEW YORK   OXFORD

OXFORD UNIVERSITY PRESS

Oxford University Press is a department of the University of Oxford.
It furthers the University's objective of excellence in research, scholarship,
and education by publishing worldwide. Oxford is a registered trade mark of
Oxford University Press in the UK and certain other countries.

Published in the United States of America by Oxford University Press
198 Madison Avenue, New York, NY 10016, United States of America.

For titles covered by Section 112 of the US Higher Education
Opportunity Act, please visit www.oup.com/us/he for the latest
information about pricing and alternate formats.

Library of Congress Cataloging-in-Publication Data
Names: Sipress, Joel M., author.
Title: The causes of the Civil War / Joel M. Sipress.
Description: New York : University of Wisconsin-Superior, [2019] | Series:
  Debating American history | Includes index.
Identifiers: LCCN 2018059163 | ISBN 9780190057084 (pbk.)
Subjects: LCSH: United States—History—Civil War, 1861–1865—Causes.
Classification: LCC E459 .S57 2019 | DDC 973.7/11—dc23 LC record available at
https://lccn.loc.gov/2018059163

Printing number: 9 8 7 6 5 4 3 2 1
Printed by LSC Communications, Inc., United States of America

TABLE OF CONTENTS

LIST OF MAPS

ABOUT THE AUTHOR

Joel M. Sipress received his PhD in United States History from the University of North Carolina at Chapel Hill. He is a Professor of History at the University of Wisconsin-Superior, where he teaches US and Latin American History. He has published articles and book chapters on the history of the US South, with a focus on the role of race and class in late nineteenth-century southern politics. He has also written essays on teaching and learning history, including "Why Students Don't Get Evidence and What We Can Do About It," *The History Teacher* 37 (May 2004): 351–363; and "The End of the History Survey Course: The Rise and Fall of the Coverage Model," coauthored with David J. Voelker, *Journal of American History* 97 (March 2011): 1050–1066, which won the 2012 Maryellen Weimer Scholarly Work on Teaching and Learning Award. He serves as co-editor of *Debating American History* with David J. Voelker.

ACKNOWLEDGMENTS

We owe gratitude to Aeron Haynie, Regan Gurung, and Nancy Chick for introducing us and pairing us to work on the Signature Pedagogies project many years ago, as well as to the UW System's Office of Professional and Instructional Development (OPID), which supported that endeavor. Brian Wheel, formerly with Oxford University Press, helped us develop the idea for *Debating American History* and started the project rolling. We want to thank Charles Cavaliere at Oxford for taking on the project and seeing it through to publication, and Anna Russell for her excellent production work. Joel thanks the University of Wisconsin–Superior for support from a sabbatical, and David thanks the University of Wisconsin–Green Bay for support from a Research Scholar grant. David would also like to thank his colleagues in humanities, history, and First Nations Studies, who have been supportive of this project for many years, and Joel thanks his colleagues in the Department of Social Inquiry. We are also indebted to our colleagues (too numerous to mention) who have advanced the Scholarship of Teaching and Learning within the field of history. Without their efforts, this project would not have been possible. We would also like the thank the reviewers of this edition: Ian Hartman, University of Alaska Anchorage; Robert J. Allison, Suffolk University, Boston; Joshua Fulton, Moraine Valley Community College; Philip Levy, University of South Florida; Ingrid Dineen-Wimberly, U of Calif., Santa Barbara and U of La Verne; Kristin Hargrove, Grossmont College; Melanie Beals Goan, University of Kentucky; Paul Hart, Texas State University; Ross A. Kennedy, Illinois State University; Scott Laderman, University of Minnesota, Duluth; John Putnam, San Diego State University; Matt Tribbe, University of Houston; Linda Tomlinson, Fayetteville State University; Shauna Hann, United States Military Academy; Michael Holm, Boston University; Raymond J. Krohn, Boise State University; Joseph Locke, University of Houston-Victoria; Ted Moore, Salt Lake Community College; Andrew L. Slap, East Tennessee State University; Matthew J. Clavin, University of Houston; Amani Marshall, Georgia State University; Luke Harlow, University of Tennessee, Knoxville; Matthew Pinsker, Dickinson College; Tyina Steptoe, University of Arizona; Daniel Vivian, University of Louisville; Melanie Benson Taylor, Dartmouth College; and Todd Romero, University of Houston.

SERIES INTRODUCTION

Although history instruction has grown richer and more varied over the past few decades, many college-level history teachers remain wedded to the coverage model, whose overriding design principle is to cover huge swaths of history, largely through the use of textbooks and lectures. The implied rationale supporting the coverage model is that students must be exposed to a wide array of facts, narratives, and concepts to have the necessary background both to be effective citizens and to study history at a more advanced level—something that few students actually undertake. Although coverage-based courses often afford the opportunity for students to encounter primary sources, the imperative to cover an expansive body of material dominates these courses, and the main assessment technique, whether implemented through objective or written exams, is to require students to identify or reproduce authorized knowledge.

Unfortunately, the coverage model has been falling short of its own goals since its very inception in the late nineteenth century. Educators and policymakers have been lamenting the historical ignorance of American youth going back to at least 1917, as Stanford professor of education Sam Wineburg documented in his illuminating exposé of the history of standardized tests of historical knowledge.[1] In 2010, the *New York Times* declared that "History is American students' worst subject," basing this judgment on yet another round of abysmal standardized test scores.[2] As we have documented in our own historical research, college professors over the past century have episodically criticized the coverage model and offered alternatives. Recently, however, college-level history instructors have been forming a scholarly community to improve the teaching of the introductory course by doing research that includes rigorous analysis of student learning. A number of historians who have become

---

1   Sam Wineburg, "Crazy for History," *Journal of American History* 90 (March 2004): 1401–1414.
2   Sam Dillon, "U.S. Students Remain Poor at History, Tests Show," *New York Times*, June 14, 2011. Accessed online at http://www.nytimes.com/2011/06/15/education/15history.html?emc=eta1&pagewanted=print.

involved in this discipline-based pedagogical research, known as the Scholarship of Teaching and Learning (SoTL), have begun to mount a challenge to the coverage model.[3]

Not only has the coverage model often achieved disappointing results by its own standards, it also proves ineffective at helping students learn how to think historically, which has long been a stated goal of history education. As Lendol Calder argued in a seminal 2006 article, the coverage model works to "cover up" or "conceal" the nature of historical thinking.[4] The eloquent lecture or the unified textbook narrative reinforces the idea that historical knowledge consists of a relatively straightforward description of the past. Typical methods of covering content hide from students not only the process of historical research—the discovery and interpretation of sources—but also the ongoing and evolving discussions among historians about historical meaning. In short, the coverage model impedes historical thinking by obscuring the fact that history is a complex, interpretative, and argumentative discourse.

Informed by SoTL, contemporary reformers have taken direct aim at the assumption that factual and conceptual knowledge must precede more sophisticated forms of historical study. Instead, reformers stress that students must learn to think historically by doing—at a novice level—what expert historians do.[5]

With these ideas in mind, we thus propose an argument-based model for teaching the introductory history course. In the argument-based model, students participate in a contested, evidence-based discourse about the human past. In other words, students are asked to argue about history. And by arguing, students develop the dispositions and habits of mind that are central to the discipline of history.[6] As the former American Historical Association (AHA) president Kenneth Pomeranz noted in late 2013, historians should consider seeing general education history courses as valuable "not for the sake of 'general

---

3 See Lendol Calder, "Uncoverage: Toward a Signature Pedagogy for the History Survey," *Journal of American History* 92 (March 2006): 1358–1370; Joel M. Sipress and David J. Voelker, "The End of the History Survey Course: The Rise and Fall of the Coverage Model," *Journal of American History* 97 (March 2011): 1050–1066; and Penne Restad, "American History Learned, Argued, and Agreed Upon," in Michael Sweet and Larry K. Michaelson, eds., *Team-Based Learning in the Social Sciences and Humanities*, 159–180 (Sterling, VA: Stylus, 2012). For an overview of the Scholarship of Teaching and Learning (SoTL) in history, see Joel M. Sipress and David Voelker, "From Learning History to Doing History: Beyond the Coverage Model," in *Exploring Signature Pedagogies: Approaches to Teaching Disciplinary Habits of Mind*, pp. 19–35, edited by Regan Gurung, Nancy Chick, and Aeron Haynie (Stylus Publishing, 2008). Note also that the International Society for the Scholarship of Teaching and Learning in History was formed in 2006. See http://www.indiana.edu/~histsotl/blog/.

4 Calder, "Uncoverage," 1362–1363.

5 For influential critiques of the "facts first" assumption, see Sam Wineburg, "Crazy for History," *Journal of American History* 90 (March 2004), 1401–1414; and Calder, "Uncoverage."

6 For discussions of argument-based courses, see Barbara E. Walvoord and John R. Breihan, "Arguing and Debating: Breihan's History Course," in Barbara E. Walvoord and Lucille P. McCarthy, *Thinking and Writing in College: A Naturalistic Study of Students in Four Disciplines* (Urbana, IL: National Council of Teachers of English, 1990), 97–143; Todd Estes, "Constructing the Syllabus: Devising a Framework for Helping Students Learn to Think Like Historians," *History Teacher* 40 (February 2007), 183–201; Joel M. Sipress, "Why Students Don't Get Evidence and What We Can Do About It," *The History Teacher* 37 (May 2004), 351–363; and David J. Voelker, "Assessing Student Understanding in Introductory Courses: A Sample Strategy," *The History Teacher* 41 (August 2008): 505–518.

knowledge' but for the intellectual operations you can teach."[7] Likewise, the AHA "Tuning Project" defines the discipline in a way much more consistent with an argument-based course than with the coverage model:

> History is a set of evolving rules and tools that allows us to interpret the past with clarity, rigor, and an appreciation for interpretative debate. It requires evidence, sophisticated use of information, and a deliberative stance to explain change and continuity over time. As a profoundly public pursuit, history is essential to active and empathetic citizenship and requires effective communication to make the past accessible to multiple audiences. As a discipline, history entails a set of professional ethics and standards that demand peer review, citation, and toleration for the provisional nature of knowledge.[8]

We have designed *Debating American History* with these values in mind.

In the coverage-based model, historical knowledge is seen as an end in itself. In the argument-based model, by contrast, the historical knowledge that students must master serves as a body of evidence to be employed in argument and debate. While the ultimate goal of the coverage approach is the development of a kind of cultural literacy, the argument-based history course seeks to develop historical modes of thinking and to encourage students to incorporate these modes of thinking into their daily lives. Particularly when housed within a broader curriculum that emphasizes engaged learning, an argument-based course prepares students to ask useful questions in the face of practical problems and challenges, whether personal, professional, or civic. Upon encountering a historical claim, such as those that frequently arise in political discussions, they will know how to ask important questions about context, evidence, and logic. In this way, the argument-based course fulfills the discipline's longstanding commitment to the cultivation of engaged and informed citizens.[9]

While there is no single correct way to structure an argument-based course, such courses do share a number of defining characteristics that drive course design.[10] In particular, argument-based courses include these elements:

1. THEY ARE ORGANIZED AROUND SIGNIFICANT HISTORICAL QUESTIONS ABOUT WHICH HISTORIANS THEMSELVES DISAGREE.

Argument-based courses are, first and foremost, question-driven courses in which "big" historical questions (rather than simply topics or themes) provide the overall organizational structure. A "big" historical question is one about which historians themselves

7   Kenneth Pomeranz, "Advanced History for Beginners: Why We Should Bring What's Best about the Discipline into the Gen Ed Classroom," *Perspectives on History* (November 2013), at http://www.historians. org/publications-and-directories/perspectives-on-history/november-2013/advanced-history-for-beginners-why-we-should-bring-what's-best-about-the-discipline-into-the-gen-ed-classroom.

8   This definition reflects the state of the Tuning Project as of September 2013. For more information, see "AHA History Tuning Project: 2013 History Discipline Core," at https://www.historians.org/teaching-and-learning/tuning-the-history-discipline/2013-history-discipline-core. Accessed January 31, 2019.

9   As recently as 2006, the AHA's Teaching Division reasserted the importance of history study and scholarship in the development of globally aware citizens. Patrick Manning, "Presenting History to Policy Makers: Three Position Papers," *Perspectives: The Newsmagazine of the American Historical Association* 44 (March 2006), 22–24.

10   Our approach to course design is deeply influenced by Grant Wiggins and Jay McTighe, *Understanding by Design*, 2nd ed. (Upper Saddle River, NJ: Pearson Education, 2006).

disagree and that has broad academic, intellectual, or cultural implications. Within these very broad parameters, the types of questions around which a course may be organized can vary greatly. The number of "big" questions addressed, however, must be relatively limited in number (perhaps 3–5 over the course of a typical fifteen-week semester) so that students can pursue the questions in depth.

2. THEY SYSTEMATICALLY EXPOSE STUDENTS TO RIVAL POSITIONS ABOUT WHICH THEY MUST MAKE INFORMED JUDGMENTS.

Argument-based courses systematically expose students to rival positions about which they must form judgments. Through repeated exploration of rival positions on a series of big questions, students see historical debate modeled in way that shatters any expectation that historical knowledge is clear-cut and revealed by authority. Students are thus confronted with the inescapable necessity to engage, consider, and ultimately evaluate the merits of a variety of perspectives.

3. THEY ASK STUDENTS TO JUDGE THE RELATIVE MERITS OF RIVAL POSITIONS ON THE BASIS OF HISTORICAL EVIDENCE.

To participate in historical argument, students must understand historical argument as more than a matter of mere opinion. For this to happen, students must learn to employ evidence as the basis for evaluating historical claims. Through being repeatedly asked to judge the relative merits of rival positions on the basis of evidence, students learn to see the relationship between historical evidence and historical assertions.

4. THEY REQUIRE STUDENTS TO DEVELOP THEIR OWN POSITIONS FOR WHICH THEY MUST ARGUE ON THE BASIS OF HISTORICAL EVIDENCE.

In an argument-based course, the ultimate aspiration should be for students to bring their own voices to bear on historical discourse in a way that is thoroughly grounded in evidence. Students must therefore have the opportunity to argue for their own positions. Such positions may parallel or synthesize those of the scholars with which they have engaged in the course or they may be original. In either case, though, students must practice applying disciplinary standards of evidence.

Learning to argue about history is, above all, a process that requires students to develop new skills, dispositions, and habits of mind. Students develop these attributes through the act of arguing in a supportive environment where the instructor provides guidance and feedback. The instructor is also responsible for providing students with the background, context, and in-depth materials necessary both to fully understand and appreciate each big question and to serve as the body of evidence that forms the basis for judgments and arguments. While argument-based courses eschew any attempt to provide comprehensive coverage, they ask students to think deeply about a smaller number of historical questions; and in the process of arguing about the selected questions, students will develop significant content knowledge in the areas emphasized.

While a number of textbooks and readers in American history incorporate elements of historical argumentation, there are no published materials available that are specifically designed to support an argument-based course. *Debating American History* consists of a series of modular units, each focused on a specific topic and question in American history that will support all four characteristics of an argument-based course noted previously. Instructors will select units that support their overall course design, perhaps incorporating one or two modules into an existing course or structuring an entire course around three to five such units. (Instructors, of course, are free to supplement the modular units with other materials of their choosing—such as additional primary documents, secondary articles, multimedia materials, and book chapters.) By focusing on a limited number of topics, students will be able to engage in in-depth historical argumentation, including consideration of multiple positions and substantial bodies of evidence.

Each unit has the following elements:

1. THE BIG QUESTION

A brief narrative introduction that poses the central question of the unit and provides general background.

2. HISTORIANS' CONVERSATIONS

This section establishes the debate by providing two or three original essays that present distinct and competing scholarly positions on the Big Question. While these essays make occasional reference to major scholars in the field, they are not intended to provide historiographical overviews but rather to provide models of historical argumentation through the presentation and analysis of evidence.

3. DEBATING THE QUESTION

Each module includes a variety of materials containing evidence for students to use to evaluate the various positions and develop a position of their own. Materials may include primary source documents, images, a timeline, maps, or brief secondary sources. The specific materials vary depending on the nature of the question. Some modules include detailed case studies that focus on a particular facet of the Big Question.

For example, one module that we have developed for an early American history course focuses on the following Big Question: "How were the English able to displace the thriving Powhatan people from their Chesapeake homelands in the seventeenth century?" The Historians' Conversations section includes two essays: "Position #1: The Overwhelming Advantages of the English"; and "Position #2: Strategic Mistakes of the Powhatans." The unit materials allow students to undertake a guided exploration of both Powhatan and English motivations and strategies. The materials include two case studies that serve specific pedagogical purposes. The first case study asks the question, "Did Pocahontas Rescue John Smith from Execution?" Answering this question requires grappling with the nature of primary sources and weighing additional evidence from secondary sources; given historians' confidence that Powhatan did adopt Smith during his captivity, the case study also raises important questions about Powhatan strategy. The second case study focuses on the 1622 surprise attack that the Powhatans (led by Opechancanough) launched against the English, posing the question: "What was the Strategy behind the 1622 Powhatan Surprise Attack?" Students wrestle with a number of scholarly perspectives regarding Opechancanough's purpose and the effectiveness of his strategy. Overall, this unit introduces students to the use of primary sources and the process of weighing different historical interpretations. Because of Disney's 1995 film *Pocahontas*, many students begin the unit thinking that they already know about the contact between the Powhatans and the English; many of them also savor the chance to bring critical, historical thinking to bear on this subject, and doing so deepens their understanding of how American Indians responded to European colonization.

Along similar lines, the Big Question for a module on the Gilded Age asks, "Why was industrialization in the late nineteenth century accompanied by such great social and political turmoil?" The materials provided allow students to explore the labor conflicts of the period as well as the Populist revolt and to draw conclusions regarding the underlying causes of the social and political upheavals. Primary sources allow students to delve into labor conflicts from the perspectives of both workers and management and to explore both Populist and anti-Populist perspectives. Three short case studies allow students to examine specific instances of social conflict in depth. A body of economic data from the late nineteenth-century is also included.

Many history instructors, when presented with the argument-based model, find its goals to be compelling, but they fear that it is overly ambitious—that introductory-level students will be incapable of engaging in historical thinking at an acceptable level. But, we must ask: how well do students learn under the coverage model? Student performance varies in an argument-based course, but it varies widely in a coverage-based course as well. In our experience, most undergraduate students are capable of achieving a basic level competence at identifying and evaluating historical interpretations and using primary and secondary sources as evidence to make basic historical arguments. We not only have evidence of this success in the form of our own grade books, but we have studied our students' learning to document the success of our approach.[11] Students can indeed learn how to think like historians at a novice level, and in doing so they will gain both an appreciation for the discipline and develop a set of critical skills and dispositions that will contribute to their overall higher education. For this to happen, however, a course must be "backwards designed" to promote and develop historical thinking. As historian Lawrence Gipson (Wabash College) asked in a 1916 AHA discussion, "Will the student catch 'historical-mindedness' from his instructor like the mumps?"[12] The answer, clearly, is "no."

In addition to the modular units focused on big questions, instructors will also be provided with a brief instructors' manual, entitled "Developing an Argument-Based Course." This volume will provide instructors with guidance and advice on course development, as

---

11 See Sipress, "Why Students Don't Get Evidence," and Voelker, "Assessing Student Understanding."

12 Lawrence H. Gipson, "Method of the Elementary Course in the Small College," *The History Teacher's Magazine* 8 (April 1917), 128. (The conference discussion took place in 1916.)

well as with sample in-class exercises and assessments. Additionally, each module includes an Instructor's Manual. Together, these resources will assist instructors with the process of creating an argument-based course, whether for a relatively small class at a liberal arts college or for a large class of students at a university. These resources can be used in both face-to-face and online courses.

The purpose of *Debating American History* is to provide instructors with both the resources and strategies that they will need to design such a course. This textbook alternative leaves plenty of room for instructor flexibility, and it requires instructors to carefully choose, organize, and introduce the readings to students, as well as to coach students through the process of thinking historically, even as they deepen their knowledge and understanding of particular eras and topics.

Joel M. Sipress
Professor of History,
University of Wisconsin-Superior

David J. Voelker
Associate Professor of Humanities and History,
University of Wisconsin-Green Bay

DEBATING AMERICAN HISTORY

THE CAUSES OF THE CIVIL WAR

THE BIG QUESTION

WHY DID CIVIL WAR ERUPT IN THE UNITED STATES IN 1861?

In the early morning hours of April 12, 1861, militiamen in Charleston, South Carolina, launched an artillery barrage against the federal garrison at Fort Sumter in the city's harbor. The early morning assault marked the climax of a months-long standoff in the southern city. Four months earlier, South Carolina (in an act known as "secession") had declared independence from the United States of America. Six other Deep South states had followed South Carolina's lead; and in February of 1861, representatives of the seven seceded states met in Montgomery, Alabama, to proclaim a new southern republic: the Confederate States of America. Both the state of South Carolina and the new Confederate government had demanded the surrender of the federal garrison at Fort Sumter. Newly elected President Abraham Lincoln, however, considered the Union to be indivisible and secession to be illegal and unconstitutional. The Confederacy, in his view, lacked any legitimate authority, and he therefore refused to relinquish control of the fort.

After thirty-three hours of bombardment, the federal troops at Sumter capitulated. Two days later, Lincoln called on the states to provide 75,000 militiamen to suppress the rebellion in the South. (At the time, the country had a very small standing army.) As a wave of patriotic fervor swept the North, men volunteered in large numbers. By contrast, four additional southern states responded to Lincoln's request by seceding and joining the Confederacy. By the summer of 1861, full-scale civil war had erupted on American soil.

The Civil War was by the far the bloodiest conflict in American history. By the time of the Confederate surrender in 1865, over 700,000 men are estimated to have perished, a toll in excess of the American fatalities in all other wars combined.[1] The Civil War touched all corners of the country, with disabled veterans (many with severed limbs) a common sight in cities and town for decades to come. The war left the United States a profoundly different place than it had been in 1860, with the primacy of the federal government fully established and the institution of slavery abolished.

As recently as the mid 1840s, few had foreseen the danger that lay just fifteen years in the future. Since winning independence from the British Empire in the 1780s, the United States had experienced explosive territorial expansion and growth in economic and political might. Americans (at least those that were free and white) generally viewed the future with confidence and had little reason to fear a national catastrophe like civil war.

---

1   J. David Hacker, "A Census-Based Count of the Civil War Dead," *Civil War History* 57 (December 2011), 311–348.

Like all nations, the United States had its internal divisions and conflicts. Prior to 1860, however, political leaders had found ways to resolve these disputes short of prolonged armed violence; and with just a few notable exceptions, the most divisive national issues had not fallen along north-south lines.

This rapid descent from exuberant optimism to bloody and destructive strife raises the question of why civil war erupted in the United States in 1861.

Historians have debated the causes of the Civil War for over a century. Some see the conflict as an outgrowth of deep, fundamental, and irreconcilable differences between North and South. Others point to the breakdown of political institutions through which compromise could have been found, or they criticize the particular choices and decisions of individual political leaders. Untangling the origins of the Civil War is extraordinarily complex but can be simplified by breaking the question down into smaller component parts. Writing in the 1940s, historian Howard K. Beale suggested that the following three questions must be addressed to arrive at a full understanding of the coming of the war:

- What caused the sectional conflict of the 1850s in which national politics polarized along north-south lines?
- What caused the secession of southern states in 1860 and 1861?
- Why did secession lead to war?[2]

THE SECTIONAL CONFLICT

Prior to the 1850s, divisive sectional issues had occasionally flared, but they had previously been resolved short of war. At the Constitutional Convention of 1787, for instance, northern and southern delegates had struggled over the basis of representation in the proposed House of Representatives. Delegates from southern states with large numbers of slaves had argued for each state to receive a number of representatives in proportion to its entire population, including those who were held in bondage. Delegates from northern states argued for representation based solely on the free population. The dispute was resolved, however, by a compromise in which representation would be based on the free population plus three-fifths of the slave population. Sectional tensions flared again in 1819 when Missouri applied to Congress for statehood under a constitution that would allow slavery. Fearful of slavery's spread, northern members of Congress demanded the gradual abolition of the institution in Missouri as a condition for statehood. Again, a compromise was found. Missouri's admission to the Union as a slave state was balanced by the admission of Maine as a free state. In addition, slavery was barred from western territories north of the 36°30' line of latitude. In the 1830s, conflict erupted over the issue of tariffs. Beginning in the 1810s, Northern manufacturing interests had successfully lobbied for high tariffs on imports to protect domestic industries like iron making from foreign competition. High tariffs, though, harmed southern cotton producers by raising prices of industrial supplies, such as iron goods, and by making it more difficult for French and English traders earn

---

2   Howard K. Beale, "What Historians Have Said About the Causes of the Civil War," in *Theory and Practice in History Study: A Report of the Committee on Historiography* (New York: Social Science Research Council, 1946), 53–102.

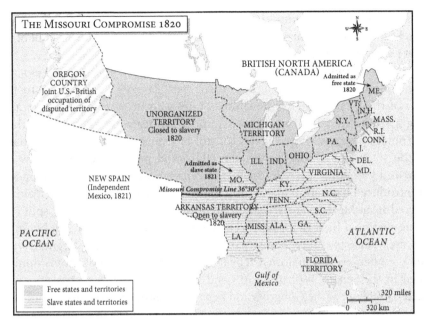

MAP 1. THE MISSOURI COMPROMISE 1820

the American money needed to purchase US cotton exports. When Congress raised tariffs again in 1828, cotton producers raised their voices in protest. Congress lowered tariffs in 1832, but some in the South remained unsatisfied. In South Carolina, a special convention declared the tariff to be null and void within the state and urged secession were the federal government to attempt to collect it. President Andrew Jackson threatened to use military force to collect tariff duties within South Carolina. Meanwhile, the Congress passed a compromise bill that further reduced tariff rates on foreign imports. Once again, a north-south confrontation was avoided.

In the 1830s, the emergence in the North of a vocal movement in favor of the abolition of slavery threatened again to stoke sectional tensions. Abolitionists pursued a variety of tactics to bring slavery to an end, including flooding Congress with anti-slavery petitions and circulating abolitionist literature in the South. Abolitionism, however, remained a minority movement even in the North and was, in fact, deeply unpopular among many northerners. In many northern communities, abolitionists faced mob violence. Some were hounded from their homes. Others had property, including printing presses, destroyed. Anti-abolitionist violence reached a peak in 1837, when a mob in the town of Alton, Illinois, attacked and murdered Elijah P. Lovejoy, a prominent anti-slavery activist.

Abolitionism, in and of itself, was insufficient to polarize the nation along north-south lines. In fact, during the 1830s and 1840s, political conflict in the United States generally followed party lines rather than sectional lines. In the 1830s, Americans had divided into two great political parties known and the Whigs and the Democrats. Both parties were national in scope with support in all corners of the country. The parties divided on a broad range of issues including economic policy and westward expansion. Both parties, however, worked to keep divisive sectional issues (such as slavery and abolitionism) out of politics. And, prior to the late 1840s, they were generally successful in doing so.

Between 1846 and 1860, the party divide between Whigs and Democrats was gradually replaced by a north-south conflict over slavery's expansion into the new territories of the West. In 1846, the United States went to war with Mexico; and after achieving a spectacular military victory, imposed a peace treaty in which the Mexican government gave the United States control of a huge swath of territory that would become the states of California, Nevada, Utah, and parts of Arizona, New Mexico, Colorado, and Wyoming. Early in the war, a Pennsylvania congressman named David Wilmot introduced legislation mandating that slavery would be excluded from any territory seized from Mexico. The so-called "Wilmot Proviso" immediately split the Congress along sectional lines, with northern Whigs and Democrats uniting behind it and southern members resisting it across party lines. The House of Representatives, where free state members were a majority, repeatedly passed the Wilmot Proviso only to see it defeated in the Senate. With the war's end in 1848, the issue of slavery's expansion consumed the energy of the Congress and began to polarize the country more generally, with some militant southerners threatening secession if slavery were excluded from the former Mexican territories.

Finally, in 1850, Congress passed a series of compromise measures designed to banish the slavery issue from national politics. California was admitted to the Union as a free state. In the rest of the former Mexican territories, though, slavery would be allowed with

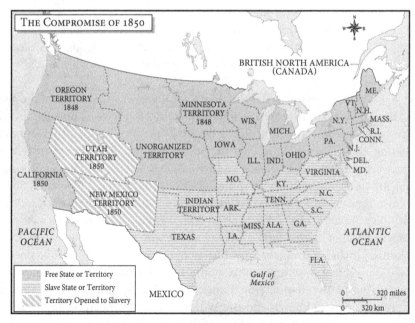

MAP 2. THE COMPROMISE OF 1850

the understanding that settlers could ban it if they so chose (a principle known as "popular sovereignty"). In addition, the Congress enacted a federal fugitive slave law to address southern complaints that northern states had been lax in returning escaped slaves to bondage, as they were required to do under the US Constitution.

The sectional truce achieved in 1850 lasted just four years. In 1854, Democratic Senator Stephen Douglas of Illinois introduced legislation to organize territorial governments in Kansas and Nebraska, where slavery was outlawed under the terms of the 1820 Missouri Compromise. Southern Democrats, however, refused to support Douglas' legislation unless the territories were opened up to slavery. To secure the votes needed for passage, Douglas agreed to the southerners' demand with the understanding that under the principle of popular sovereignty, settlers in Kansas and Nebraska could exclude slavery if they so chose. The Kansas-Nebraska Act, which amounted to a repeal of the Missouri Compromise, unleashed a storm of protest across the North. From that point onward, the slavery extension issue came to dominate politics in both the North and the South, with more and more northerners demanding that slavery be kept out of the western territories and southern slave owners demanding the right to carry their human property anywhere in the territories of the west. Those who sought a middle ground found themselves squeezed between the two polarized positions.

By 1860, sectionally polarized politics had replaced the earlier Whig-Democrat divide. The Whig Party collapsed in the early 1850s. In the North, the vacuum left by the demise of the Whigs was filled by the newly established Republican Party, a party's whose central principle was that slavery should not be allowed to expand beyond the states where it

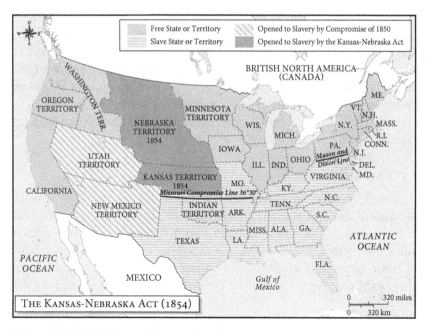

MAP 3. THE KANSAS-NEBRASKA ACT (1854)

already existed. The Republicans won support not just from former Whigs but also from former Democrats concerned that the Democratic Party had fallen too much under the influence of southern slave owners. By 1856, the Republicans were the dominant party in the northern states; and in 1860, their presidential nominee, Abraham Lincoln, rode strong support in the North to the White House on a platform of preventing the expansion of slavery. Lincoln received a solid majority of the vote in the free states. The Republicans, by contrast, did not even campaign in most of the slave states, and their candidate received not a single vote in the Deep South.

SECESSION

The sectional polarization of American politics would not have resulted in war had it not culminated in the secession of seven southern states from the Union. Immediately after Lincoln's election in November 1860, southern militants began to agitate for secession, with one South Carolina newspaper declaring, "The tea has been thrown overboard; the revolution of 1860 has been initiated."[3] And, indeed, it was South Carolina that set the pace. Four days after Lincoln's election, the South Carolina legislature called for a special state convention to be held in December for the purpose of considering secession. On December 20, 1860, the South Carolina convention voted unanimously to declare independence from the United States of America. Outside of South Carolina, advocates of immediate secession faced more vocal opposition. Nonetheless, by the beginning of February, an additional six Deep South states (Georgia, Alabama, Florida, Mississippi, Louisiana, and Texas) had declared independence. Delegates from the seven seceded states gathered in Montgomery, Alabama, in early February and established the Confederate States of America.

Advocates of independence, however, were disappointed when none of the eight remaining slave states acted to join the Confederacy. A number of states (including North Carolina and Tennessee) refused to even call secession conventions. In Arkansas, Missouri, and Virginia, conventions did meet but rejected secession. When Abraham Lincoln was inaugurated as President on March 4, 1861, he thus faced a highly fluid and uncertain situation. While seven southern states had voted themselves out of the Union, there was reason to believe that the secessionist wave had crested and that a solution to the crisis short of war might be possible.

LINCOLN'S OPTIONS

Between Lincoln's election in November 1860 and his inauguration the following March, members of Congress sought a compromise that could bring a peaceful resolution to the secession crisis. Kentucky Senator John J. Crittenden, for instance, proposed re-establishing the Missouri Compromise line and allowing slavery in the territories south of the line while banning it to the north. Others suggested adopting a constitutional amendment to explicitly bar the federal government from interfering with the institution

---

3   David M. Potter, *The Impending Crisis, 1848–1861* (New York: Harper and Row, 1976), 485.

of slavery in states where it already existed. President-elect Lincoln encouraged Republicans to consider concessions that might reassure southern slave owners; but on the key issue of the expansion of slavery, he urged Republicans to stand firm. The Republicans had been elected on a promise to keep slavery out of the western territories, and Lincoln refused to back down from that promise. In the end, a compromise solution could not be found. The President-elect, however, did repeatedly assure southern slave owners that he had neither the intention nor (in his view) the constitutional authority to interfere with slavery in states where it already existed. In late December of 1860, for instance, he wrote to Alexander Stephens of Georgia, an old political colleague and friend: "Do the people of the South really entertain fears that a Republican administration would, directly, or indirectly, interfere with their slaves, or with them, about their slaves? If they do, I wish to assure you, as once a friend, and still, I hope, not an enemy, that there is no cause for such fears."[4]

In his March 4 inauguration speech, Lincoln affirmed that he would not interfere with slavery in the southern states, but he also proclaimed the Union to be indivisible and declared acts of violence against the authority of the United States to be "insurrectionary or revolutionary." No state, he explained, could lawfully leave the Union; and he, as President, had the responsibility to faithfully execute federal law in all the states, even those that claimed to be independent. Lincoln, though, promised to refrain from the use of force unless the rebels themselves initiated armed conflict.

In the face of secession, Lincoln and the Republicans had rejected both the option of compromise and the option of peaceful separation. Having rejected these two options, war soon became inevitable. And, just over a month after Lincoln's inauguration, war came when Confederate forces opened fire on the federal garrison at Fort Sumter in Charleston Harbor.

WHY DID CIVIL WAR ERUPT IN 1861?

Why did Civil War erupt in the United States in 1861? To answer that question, the following must be explained:

- Why did national politics polarize along sectional lines? During the 1830s and 1840s, political conflict in the United States had fallen along party lines. The Whigs and Democrats were both national parties with support in all corners of the country. The two parties worked to keep divisive sectional issues (like slavery) out of politics. Why was the Whig-Democratic divide of earlier times replaced by an increasingly bitter North-South divide in the 1850s?
- Following the election of Republican presidential candidate Abraham Lincoln in 1860, seven Deep South states declared independence from the United States. If not for the secession of these states, the sectional conflict of the 1850s would not have led to war. Why did the states of the Deep South secede from the Union?

---

4   Abraham Lincoln to Alexander Stephens, December 22, 1860, in Roy P. Basler, ed., *The Collected Works of Abraham Lincoln*, vol. 4 (New Brunswick, NJ: Rutgers University Press, 1953–1955), 160–161.

- Why did Lincoln and the Republicans reject both compromise and peaceable separation? Secession did not make war inevitable. Between Lincoln's election and his inauguration, members of Congress sought a political compromise to peacefully resolve the secession crisis. Why did Lincoln and the Republicans reject compromise on the single most divisive issue—the expansion of slavery into western territories? And why did they not simply allow the seven seceded states to go in peace?

TIMELINE

1820
Missouri Compromise adopted by Congress. Missouri admitted to the Union as a slave state. Slavery banned from western territories north of the 36°30' line of latitude.

Late 1820s and 1830s
Emergence of an active abolitionist movement in the northern states. Mob violence against abolitionists in parts of the North.

1846
Outbreak of the Mexican-American War. The United States invades northern Mexico. Pennsylvania Congressman David Wilmot introduces legislation to bar slavery from any territory seized from Mexico.

1848
Conclusion of Mexican-American War. Mexico cedes huge swath of territory to the United States. Congress deadlocks over issue of whether slavery will be allowed in the region and is unable to organize territorial governments there.

1850
Compromise of 1850 approved by the Congress. California admitted to the Union as a free state. Slavery allowed in remainder of the Mexican territories with the understanding that settlers could ban it if they so chose ("popular sovereignty"). A strong federal fugitive slave act approved.

1852–1856
Collapse of the Whig Party as a national organization.

1854
Congress approves the Kansas-Nebraska Act allowing slavery north of the 36°30´ line of latitude under the principle of popular sovereignty. Wave of protest across the North. Founding of the Republican Party on a "free soil" platform of preventing the expansion of slavery. Southern political leaders increasingly unite behind the demand that slave owners be allowed to carry their human property throughout the western territories.

1856
Fighting erupts between pro- and anti-slavery settlers in the Kansas Territory. Caning of Senator Charles Sumner. Republican presidential candidate John C. Frémont carries the majority of the northern vote in the November election as a "free soil" candidate.

1857
Supreme Court's Dred Scott decision declares the Missouri Compromise unconstitutional and legalizes slavery in all the federal territories.

1858–1860
Southern demands for federal legislation to protect slave property in the territories grow.

1860
Presidential election. Democratic Party splits into northern and southern wings, each of which nominates its own presidential candidate. Republican candidate Abraham Lincoln sweeps the North on a promise to prevent the expansion of slavery and is elected president.

1860 (December 20)
South Carolina secedes from the United States.

1861 (January–February)
Six additional southern states secede. Members of Congress search for a compromise to resolve the crisis.

1861 (February 9)
Representatives from the seceded states establish the Confederate States of America.

1861 (March 4)
Lincoln inaugurated President. Reaffirms that he will not interfere with the institution of slavery where it already exists. Declares secession to be an act of insurrection, but promises to refrain from applying force unless the rebels themselves initiate armed conflict.

1861 (March 5)
Lincoln is informed that the federal garrison at Fort Sumter in Charleston, South Carolina harbor had only several weeks of supplies remaining.

1861 (April 6)
Lincoln dispatches message to South Carolina governor stating that an attempt to resupply the Fort Sumter garrison with provisions only would be made.

1861 (April 11)
Confederate forces demand surrender of Fort Sumter.

1861 (April 12)
Confederate artillery commences attack on Fort Sumter.

1861 (April 14)
Federal garrison at Fort Sumter surrenders.

1861 (April 15)
President Lincoln issues a call for 75,000 state militia to enter federal service to suppress the rebellion.

1861 (April–June)
Four additional states secede and join the Confederacy.

HISTORIANS' CONVERSATIONS

POSITION #1—THE AMERICAN CIVIL WAR:

Two Cultures, Separate and Hostile

At the time of the American Revolution, the United States was comprised of a group of sparsely populated former colonies hugging the Atlantic Ocean. The vast majority of Americans earned their livelihoods from the land. Outside of a handful of seaports with close ties to Europe, life revolved around face-to-face relationships developed over the course of a lifetime in small, isolated, rural communities. The urban and industrial revolutions that had begun to reshape England had barely touched the United States, if at all. The two largest cities, New York and Philadelphia, had populations of just 25,000 each. The nation's total population was under three million. In many ways, Americans lived lives that were little changed from those of their European forbears generations earlier.

By 1860, the United States had been transformed. In a demographic revolution virtually unprecedented in human history, the nation's population expanded to over thirty million, and settlement expanded westward beyond the Mississippi River. Fed by rapid industrial and commercial development, great cities arose. Railroads and canals tied isolated rural communities together and forged a truly national economy. The invention of the telegraph allowed near-instantaneous communications. In the local newspaper, a farm family in a western state like Illinois could stay current with the latest political news from Washington, DC, or the fashionable trends from New York. These changes, however, did not affect all regions equally. While the northern states embraced these developments, the slave states of the South retained their agrarian character. Thus, by 1860, the United States was home to two divergent and increasingly incompatible cultures. It is in the conflict of a traditional South and a modernizing North that the origins of the American Civil War are to be found.

Statistical comparisons make plain the degree to which the two sections had diverged by 1860. At the time of the Revolution, about 5% of Americans lived in urban areas (defined as cities and towns with a population of five thousand or more) with little difference between the North and the South. In 1860, by contrast, 26% of the free-state population lived in urban areas, while just 10% of those in slave states did so.[1] Charleston, South Carolina, one of the leading cities of the colonial era with a population rivaling Boston's, had grown to just 41,000 by the time of the Civil War. Meanwhile, Boston had become a

---

1   James M. McPherson, *Ordeal by Fire: The Civil War and Reconstruction* (New York: Alfred A. Knopf, 1982), 24.

major metropolis with a population nearing 200,000; Philadelphia had surpassed a half a million; and New York City was approaching the one million mark. Virginia, the most populous of the thirteen colonies, had been surpassed by New York (now with more than twice Virginia's population), Pennsylvania, Ohio, and even the relatively new western state of Illinois. New Orleans, with a population of 169,000, was the only true metropolitan center in the Confederacy. The Crescent City's growth, though, was fueled largely by the trade in foodstuffs shipped down the Mississippi River from Midwestern states like Ohio, Indiana, and Illinois. The Midwest itself had seen major cities sprout up seemingly overnight. Cincinnati, Ohio, was nearing the 200,000 mark; and Chicago, established just two decades earlier, had surpassed 100,000 residents, larger than any city in the Confederacy except for New Orleans. The growth and urbanization of the northern states was driven by rapid industrial and commercial development. In 1810, almost one-third of the manufacturing in the United States was located in the slave states; yet by the Civil War, the free states held 84% of the nation's total manufacturing. Massachusetts, New York, and Pennsylvania each produced more manufactured goods than the entire eleven states of the Confederacy, with New York and Pennsylvania alone each more than doubling Confederate output.[2]

The institution of slavery retarded the commercial and industrial development of the South. In the North, investment capital was originally held mainly by merchants in coastal port cities who had a vested interest in promoting trade and commerce. With the emergence of new technologies and production methods, these merchants began to reinvest their profits in manufacturing industries such as textiles, clothing, and shoes. Soon, the burgeoning manufacturing sector of the northern states took on a momentum of its own, as investors aggressively sought opportunities for profit through the production of a wide range of goods. In the 1830s, capital began to flow into railroad construction, and soon the agricultural west and urbanizing east were bound together by a national rail network that created new markets for both farm products and manufactured goods. In the southern states, by contrast, investment capital flowed primarily into land and slaves rather than into new manufacturing industries. The South witnessed its own railroad boom in the 1850s, but the lines that were built were designed primarily to facilitate the export of cotton to the industrializing North and to Europe. Southern railroad development thus created even greater incentives for money to flow into the plantation economy.

The economic distinctions between North and South did not, in and of themselves, make a civil war inevitable. As Bertram Wyatt-Brown points out, "Differing economic systems may coexist peaceably in the same country. But when moral assumptions diverge, the chances for disunion are much greater."[3] But the divergent economic paths pursed by the two sections did ultimately give rise to cultural and moral systems that were increasingly in conflict. In the South, life continued to revolve around the local community. Meanwhile, modern communications and transportation technologies encouraged northerners to forge identities that transcended local boundaries. Literacy rates and educational levels

---

2   James M. McPherson, "Antebellum Southern Exceptionalism: A New Look at an Old Question," *Civil War History* 29 (September 1983), 237.

3   Bertram Wyatt-Brown, *Southern Honor: Ethics and Behavior in the Old South* (New York: Oxford University Press, 1982), 24.

in the North were among the highest in the world. In the free states, 94% of adults could read and write, and 72% of those aged 5–19 were enrolled in school. In the slave states, by contrast, just 83% of free adults were literate, and 35% of the free population aged 5–19 were enrolled in school. Including the enslaved (who were generally barred by law from learning to read and write), the southern literacy rate was approximately 50%. Per capita magazine circulation among white southerners was also less than half of that among northerners.[4] In the South, identity flowed from one's position within the local social hierarchy. Status and "honor" (one's good name and reputation) counted for more than wealth and profit. This emphasis on social standing encouraged the southern elite to pursue the acquisition of land and slaves at the expense of commercial and industrial development, as status flowed to those who held membership in the region's plantation aristocracy. Meanwhile, the North was growing more individualistic, with geographic and social mobility, individual achievement, and success in business enterprise increasingly prized. The divergent moral worldviews of the two sections can be illustrated by their contrasting approaches toward issues of social control and violence. In the North, inter-personal violence came to be seen as evidence of a lack of self-control. Southerners, by contrast, retained their traditional attachment to martial values. The practice of dueling persisted in the southern states even as it died out in the North. Even as law enforcement in the North began to professionalize, in the South, social control remained the responsibil-ity of the white men at large, exemplified by the institution of the slave patrol. Southerners were more likely to volunteer for military service, and the army's officer corps was drawn disproportionately from the region. All but one of the country's private military colleges were found in the South.[5]

The agrarian culture of the South was deeply conservative, with tradition prized over innovation. By contrast, northerners increasingly identified change with "progress." As the cultures of the two sections diverged, northerners and southerners came to view each other with suspicion and disdain. Many in the South saw northerners as grasping, mate-rialistic, and dishonorable. In 1861, for instance, one South Carolinian told a travelling journalist from England, "We are an agricultural people, pursuing our own system, and working out our own destiny, breeding up women and men with some other purpose than to make them vulgar, fanatical, cheating Yankees."[6] Northerners, in turn, increasingly saw the South as backward and primitive. As a young man, Republican Senator William H. Seward of New York had travelled through Virginia and wrote of "exhausted soil, old and decaying towns, wretchedly-neglected roads, and, in every respect, an absence of enterprise and improvement." Years later, in his famed "Irrepressible Conflict" speech, Seward declared that slave labor was antithetical to both democratic self-government and to the development of the nation.[7] Charles Colcock Jones Jr., a Georgia politician who had studied at northern universities, summed up the growing sectional divide bluntly.

---

4   McPherson, *Ordeal by Fire*, 23–25.
5   McPherson, "Antebellum Southern Exceptionalism," 239–140.
6   Quoted in McPherson, "Antebellum Southern Exceptionalism," 233.
7   Frederick W. Seward, *William H. Seward: An Autobiography* (New York: Derby and Miller, 1891), 268; William H. Seward, "The Irrepressible Conflict," in David J. Brewer, ed., *The World's Best Orations*, Vol. 9 (St. Louis, MO: Fred P. Kaiser, 1899), 3395–3396.

"In this country have arisen two races which, although claiming a common parentage, have been so entirely separated by climate, by morals, by religion, and by estimates so totally opposite to all that constitutes honor, truth, and manliness, that they cannot longer exist under the same government."[8]

The slavery controversy was simply the spark for the sectional conflict. For southerners, the slavery issue was but a manifestation of what they saw as a broader assault on their way of life. As Bertram Wyatt-Brown points out, the economics of slavery alone cannot explain why white southerners, most of whom were non-slave owners, were willing to both shed and give blood during the Civil War.[9] Republican promises to respect the institution of slavery where it already existed rang hollow to southerners, as such promises were accompanied by moral denunciations of the slavery that, for southerners, were an intolerable challenge to their honor. Had the power and influence of the two sections remained roughly balanced, the breach could perhaps have been avoided. The growing population and economic might of the North, however, produced a sense of confidence in the free states that bordered on arrogance and a defensiveness in the slave states that bordered on paranoia. For northerners, the material progress of the free states demonstrated the self-evident superiority of their way of life. For those in the South, the growing might of the free states, and the spread of anti-southern sentiment within them, fostered a sense of second-class status that they simply could not abide. For southerners, the election of Abraham Lincoln to the Presidency in 1860 was evidence that power and influence within the nation had shifted to those who disrespected them, their institutions, and their way of life. Both their honor and their sense of self-preservation required them to pursue independence. As James McPherson writes, "Southerners believed that survival of their special civilization could be assured only in a separate nation. The creation of the Confederacy was merely a political ratification of an irrevocable separation that had already taken place in the hearts and minds of the people."[10]

---

8   Quoted in McPherson, "Antebellum Southern Exceptionalism," 233.
9   Brown, *Southern Honor*, xviii.
10 McPherson, "Antebellum Southern Exceptionalism," 234.

POSITION #2—SLAVERY AND ITS ROLE IN THE AMERICAN CIVIL WAR

When a nation-state descends into bloody and destructive civil war, as did the United States between 1861 and 1865, it is common to attribute the conflict to deep and irreconcilable cultural distinctions among the nation's people. Nations, we are told, are held together by bonds of common culture. Thus, when they unravel, it must be due to the absence of such bonds. In the wake of Yugoslavia's collapse in the 1990s, for example, we were regaled with tales of the "ancient" enmity between Serbs and Croatians that doomed that nation from the start. Or, in the case of Iraq, we are told that divisions between Shia and Sunni Muslims and between Arabic and Kurdish speakers were virtually insurmountable barriers to the construction of a stable national government. Similarly, it is common for scholars to attribute the American Civil War to a deep and fundamental cultural divide between North and South—distinctions, we are told, that over time produced two separate and increasingly hostile civilizations on American soil.[1] The North, we are told, was urban and industrial. The South, by contrast, was agrarian. The North was egalitarian; the South aristocratic. The North was entrepreneurial and open to change; the South was traditional and conservative. The North was individualistic; the South communal. The North was Puritan in religious sentiments; the South evangelical. And so on.

In reality, all but the smallest of nation-states are characterized by significant internal diversity. Only in the wake of great civil conflagrations does such diversity come to be seen as a barrier to national unity. The civil conflict then becomes its own evidence for the depth of the supposed cultural divide. This was true of both Yugoslavia and Iraq, and it was also true of the United States. As Edward Pessen points out, the American Civil War heightened perceptions of "supposedly irreconcilable differences" and helped to popularize interpretations of US history that emphasized the cultural antitheses between North and South.[2] In reality, however, for virtually every difference between the sections, a parallel commonality can be found. Despite the beginnings of urbanization and industrialization, the North remained primarily agrarian in 1860. And, despite the impressions created by films and novels like "Gone with the Wind," wealthy planters were but a tiny fraction of the white population of the South. Most white southerners were non-slave owning family farmers who had much in common with their northern counterparts. The institution of

---

1 For an example of this view, see James M. McPherson, "Antebellum Southern Exceptionalism: A New Look at an Old Question," *Civil War History* 29 (September 1983), 230–244.

2 Edward Pessen, "How Different from Each Other Were the Antebellum North and South?" *American Historical Review* 85 (December 1980), 1120–1121.

slavery, it is true, was limited to the southern states. The North, however, had its own racial caste system in which African American people faced daily discrimination and, in most states, lacked basic civil and political rights, including the right to vote. Even the institution of slavery itself, as Steven Hahn points out, was in many ways a national rather than a sectional institution, with northern commercial and manufacturing interests deeply enmeshed with the cotton economy of the South.[3] The search for cultural antitheses between North and South also serves to mask the significant regional diversity within both sections. While northeastern states like Massachusetts and New York had witnessed significant urbanization and industrialization by 1860, Midwestern states, like Illinois and Wisconsin, retained many of the characteristics of the frontier. The contrast between the plantation regions of the South, dominated by large landholdings and slave labor, and the so-called upcountry South, in which small family farms predominated, was equally stark.

Cultural distinctions cannot, in and of themselves, explain the sudden eruption of sectional strife in the 1850s and its culmination in secession and war in 1861. As David Potter writes, "To explain an antagonism which sprang up suddenly, and died down suddenly, the historian does not need to discover, and cannot effectively use, a factor which has been constant over a long period, as the cultural difference between the North and South has been."[4] As recently as the 1840s, Americans North and South had shared a fervent nationalism that helped fuel the rapid territorial expansion of the United States. And in the Spanish-American War of 1898 and the First World War (which the United States entered in 1917), southerners eagerly fought for the very nation against which many of their parents and grandparents had rebelled. Cultural diversity, Potter points out, only generates civil conflict when "it has been translated into opposing policies for dealing with a particular question."[5] One undeniable distinction between the North and South was the centrality of the institution of slavery to the economic and political interests of the dominant elites within the southern states. It was only when southern slaveholders came to perceive a fundamental threat to their interests that a conflict along sectional lines became inevitable.

The most direct threat to the institution of slavery was the growing abolitionist movement that spread across the North in the mid-nineteenth century. Although anti-slavery sentiment dated back to the colonial era, only in the 1820s and 1830s did an organized movement advocating the immediate abolition of the institution emerge in the United States. Abolitionism drew its greatest support from evangelical Christian social reformers who considered slavery a sin, and from the free black population of the North. In 1829, a black Boston resident named David Walker published a pamphlet (entitled *Walker's Appeal to the Colored Citizens of the World*) urging southern slaves to rise up against the institution of slavery. Shortly thereafter, white social reformer and editor William Lloyd Garrison commenced publication of a weekly anti-slavery newspaper entitled *The Liberator*. In 1833, Garrison helped found the American Anti-Slavery Society, which for the next several decades remained a steadfast and influential voice for the immediate abolition of slavery. Abolitionists pursued a variety of

---

3   Steven Hahn, *A Nation Without Borders: The United States and Its World in an Age of Civil Wars, 1830–1910* (New York: Viking, 2016), 3.

4   David M. Potter, *The South and the Sectional Conflict* (Baton Rouge: Louisiana State University Press, 1968), 78.

5   Ibid. 80.

tactics, ranging from public protest meetings and petition campaigns to running candidates for office. The movement made particularly effective use of literature to reach the broader public. Escaped slaves, such as Frederick Douglass and Harriet Jacobs, published riveting accounts of the horrors they had endured under bondage. Harriet Beecher Stowe's anti-slavery novel, *Uncle Tom's Cabin* (published in 1852), sold 300,000 copies in its first year and went on to become the second best-selling book of nineteenth century—second only to the Bible.

Prior to the Civil War, abolitionism never commanded majority support among northerners. In fact, abolitionists faced ostracism and even mob violence in many communities. The spread of anti-slavery sentiment nonetheless posed a significant threat to the institution of slavery. Maintaining control over a subject population of four million (about one-third of the population of the eleven Confederate states) required constant vigilance and a united front among white southerners, both slave owners and non-slave owners. Despite protestations to the contrary, defenders of slavery were aware of the fragility of the institution. Incidents such as the 1831 Nat Turner rebellion, which left about sixty white Virginians dead before it was suppressed, were reminders that the enslaved were not the content and docile population that southern apologists claimed. The steady trickle of runaways who escaped to freedom in the North and in Canada was a further reminder. To prevent acts of resistance and rebellion, southern states enacted legislation declaring it illegal to teach a slave to read and write, required the permission of their masters (documented in a pass) for a slave to travel freely through countryside, and organized armed patrols to keep a watch for runaways and other potential "troublemakers."

Slavery's fragility explains the seeming paranoia with which southerners responded to the emergence of abolitionism. From the perspective of slave owners, any crack in the pro-slavery national consensus, particularly one that might expose slaves themselves to dangerous ideas regarding freedom and the possibility of emancipation, was a dire threat. When abolitionists began to circulate anti-slavery pamphlets through the southern mails, mobs in many areas confiscated and destroyed the offending literature. States such as Louisiana passed legislation outlawing speeches or writings that might promote discontent among the free black population and insubordination among slaves. When abolitionist petitions began to pour into the US Congress in the 1830s, southern representatives were incensed. At the insistence of pro-slavery forces, the House of Representatives imposed a "gag rule" that prohibited the body from discussing or even receiving such petitions.

Ironically, the very lengths to which southerners went to defend their "peculiar institution" helped to spread anti-slavery sentiment in the North beyond the confines of the committed abolitionists. Over time, many in the North who had little concern for the plight of the enslaved began to see the institution of slavery and those who presided over it as threats to their own interests and rights. The congressional gag rule, for many northerners, symbolized slave owners' lack of respect for basic constitutional rights, a perception confirmed by the savage beating of Massachusetts Senator Charles Sumner in the halls of Congress by South Carolina Congressman Preston Brooks in 1856. The aggressive tactics employed by slave catchers seeking fugitives in the North prompted a number of states to enact "personal liberty laws" designed to protect the due process rights of individuals accused of being escapees from bondage. It was the insistence of southerners that they be allowed to carry their human property into the new territories of the West, though, that prompted the greatest outrage in the North, particularly among those who feared that western lands would be gobbled up by slave owners at the expense of potential northern settlers. By 1860, northern hostility to slavery and slave owners was sufficiently widespread to propel Republican candidate Abraham Lincoln to the White House on a "free soil" platform that promised to arrest the spread of the institution of slavery and place it on its path toward its ultimate demise.

Abraham Lincoln was not an abolitionist. His hope was that the institution could be gradually and voluntarily eliminated; and as President, he promised to respect slavery where it already existed. The rise to power of an anti-slavery Republican Party was nevertheless a catastrophe for slave-owning interests. Since the foundation of the republic, southerners had held disproportionate power within the national government. A majority of Speakers of the House of Representatives and Supreme Court justices had hailed from the South. Southern slave owners had also occupied the White House for a majority of the years since independence. Northern presidents generally had strong political ties to southern slaveholding interests.[6] The influence that southerners wielded in Washington assured them that the power of the federal government would be used to buttress the institution of slavery rather than undermine it. The election of Lincoln marked a radical shift in sectional power that alone would have raised concerns in the South. More troubling, though, was the fact that the newly elected President represented a political party, the Republicans, that was openly hostile toward slavery and that envisioned the gradual elimination of the institution from American soil.

Lincoln's election sparked an intense debate within the South over how to best secure slavery's future. Advocates of secession argued that the Republican Party represented a clear and present danger to the institution. Republicans, they warned, would appoint enemies of slavery to the federal courts and as federal marshals. They would fail to enforce the fugitive slave clause of the United States Constitution, which required the federal government to return those who had escaped north to their masters. They would use the influence of the federal government to spread the Republican Party to the South, thus undermining the institution of slavery from within. And, in the worst case scenario, they could not be relied on to wield the military might of the United States to suppress slave rebellions. Only through independence, secessionists argued, could slavery's future be made secure. Southern Unionists generally agreed that the Republican Party was a threat to slavery. They maintained, however, that the constitutional division of powers provided sufficient protection for the institution and that secession should be employed only as a last resort should the Republicans overstep their constitutional bounds.

The advocates of immediate secession carried the day in the states of the Deep South, and the result was a bloody and destructive civil war. In the wake of that conflict, scholars searched for deep and irreconcilable cultural differences between the sections to explain a struggle that left over 700,000 people dead. After all, what else could explain the willingness of so many to kill and to die for their respective causes? As David Potter writes, however, "The American Civil War must be interpreted less in terms of antitheses and dissimilarities between North and South, and more in terms of the prolonged sequence of

---

6   James M. McPherson, *Ordeal by Fire: The Civil War and Reconstruction* (New York: Alfred A. Knopf, 1982), 132.

interest conflicts which crystallized along sectional lines."[7] The slaveholding elites of the southern states came to believe that the spread of anti-slavery sentiment and the rise of the Republican Party posed a dire threat to their economic and political interests. In response, they led the South into secession and war. Their gamble failed. The United States was preserved and slavery was abolished, but only at the cost of countless thousands.

---

7   Potter, *Sectional Conflict*, 80.

POSITION #3—THE "IRREPRESSIBLE CONFLICT" RECONSIDERED:

Party Breakdown and the Coming of the Civil War

In his famous 1858 speech, Republican Senator (and future Secretary of State) William H. Seward spoke of an "irrepressible conflict" between the opposing and enduring forces of free and slave labor. The United States, he explained, could not permanently remain half slave and half free. Eventually, either free or slave labor would triumph throughout the nation. Seward's speech has sometimes been misread as a prophecy of civil war. In fact, Seward both believed and hoped that the institution of slavery would gradually wither and eventually die were its opponents able to prevent its expansion. When the secession crisis erupted in the wake of the Abraham Lincoln's election to the presidency, Seward was among the Republican politicians most intent on finding a compromise solution that would preserve the nation while avoiding a military conflict.

Nonetheless, for many historians, Seward's "irrepressible conflict" has served as a powerful metaphor for a view of the American Civil War that sees it as the result of an inevitable and unavoidable confrontation between two antagonistic social systems. Slavery, they argue, was an anachronism in a nation firmly on a path toward a modern industrial future in which there would be no place for antiquated forms of servile labor. With population growth and economic development steadily shifting the nation's center of political gravity northward, and with slavery on the decline throughout the western world, southern slaveholding interests became increasingly defensive and protective of the region's "peculiar institution." The Republican electoral victory of 1860 marked a fundamental shift in power that, if not contested, would seal slavery's long-term fate. For these historians, secession was a counter-revolution against the burgeoning forces of modernity that were sweeping the United States and that would eventually transform the entire globe. The triumph of the Union, in this view, represented the victory of a modernity that had no place for the institution of slavery.[1]

It requires a significant leap of logic, however, to argue that the American Civil War was made inevitable by the gradual worldwide decline of slavery and other forms of bound labor. By 1900, slavery had indeed been abolished throughout the Americas; but for the most part, this goal was achieved without resort to violence. (The Haitian Revolution is an obvious exception to this pattern.) In the British Caribbean, slavery was abolished

---

1 For an example of this view, see James M. McPherson, "Antebellum Southern Exceptionalism: A New Look at an Old Question," *Civil War History* 29 (September 1983), 230–244.

through an 1833 act of the British Parliament. In Brazil, the national legislature abolished slavery in 1888 via the so-called "Golden Law." In neither case did slave owners and their allies take up arms to defend the institution. The particular timing of the American Civil War, as well, must be explained. Slavery had been a subject of controversy at the national level from the very founding of the republic, and disputes involving the institution had flared up on a regular basis. Prior to the 1850s, though, political leaders had found ways to resolve these conflicts through negotiation and compromise. As Michael Holt writes, "What produced the sectional hostility . . . was not necessarily what caused armed conflict in 1861. Ideological differences, after all, do not always produce wars."[2]

As William Gienapp points out, the United States Congress (which brought together northern and southern representatives) had been the traditional place where intersectional compromises were worked out.[3] The Missouri controversy of 1819–1821, the nullification crisis of 1833, and the conflict in the late 1840s over the status of slavery in the territories taken from Mexico, for instance, had all been resolved through congressional compromises. In the 1850s, by contrast, congressional leaders found it increasingly difficult to arrive at mutually acceptable solutions to sectional controversies. Ultimately, the secession crisis of 1860–1861 proved insoluble, and the result was war. What needs explanation is why, in the 1850s, compromise solutions to the controversies surrounding slavery could no longer be found; and why, unlike elsewhere in the Americas, slavery's gradual decline could not be managed peacefully, as Republican leaders like Seward expected and hoped for.

The answers to these questions are to be found in a radical shift in the nation's political parties that took place in the decade before the Civil War. Prior to the 1850s, American politics was dominated by two great national parties, the Whigs and the Democrats, both of which had substantial support in all regions of the country. Within each party, political leaders forged political alliances that transcended sectional lines and developed personal relationships with party-mates from other regions. Whigs and Democrats, regardless of region, had a strong incentive to strike sectional compromises to maintain the unity of their respective parties and to maintain their relationships with allies from other parts of the country. With the sudden collapse of the Whigs in the early 1850s and the gradual decline of Northern Democrats over the course of the decade, the cross-sectional pattern of national politics was disrupted. Out of this void emerged a new style of politics in which candidates and parties appealed to voters by championing the perceived interests of the North and South. In this new political environment, there was little incentive to find solutions to sectional controversies. On the contrary, sectional defiance was rewarded politically while compromise was punished.

A healthy political party system requires conflict and controversy to thrive. Controversial public issues provide each party with a basis on which to appeal to voters and to mobilize support. In the absence of public controversy, political participation wanes as voters find little reason to engage with the electoral system. In the 1830s, the Democratic and Whig Parties organized themselves at the national level in support and opposition to the

---

2   Michael F. Holt, *The Political Crisis of the 1850s* (New York: John Wiley and Sons, 1978), 2.

3   William E. Gienapp, "The Crisis of American Democracy: The Political System and the Coming of the Civil War," in *Why the Civil War Came*, ed. Gabor S. Boritt (New York: Oxford University Press, 1996), 84.

administration of Democratic President Andrew Jackson. For Democrats, Jackson was the champion of the common man. He was an Indian fighter who had pushed aggressively to open up the West for white settlement. He was the enemy of corruption who had taken on the powerful financial interests behind the Second Bank of the United States. He was the advocate of a limited government that would leave citizens to live their lives free from outside interference. For Whigs, by contrast, Jackson was a tyrant who had overstepped his constitutional bounds (particularly in his battle against the Second Bank of the United States) and who had pursued reckless and irresponsible policies that were damaging to the country. Whigs offered themselves to voters as advocates of commercial development who, unlike the Democrats, were eager to invest public resources in building the transportation and financial infrastructure necessary to make the United States a wealthy and powerful nation.

By the 1850s, the passions unleashed by the Jackson Administration had cooled, and the political positions of the parties had converged. Democrats became increasingly willing to employ public resources to help finance transportation projects such as railroads. Whigs, in turn, embraced the goal of national expansion, with only a handful of the party's representatives in Congress opposing the American war against Mexico. Increasingly, the Whig Party suffered from its difficulties in distinguishing itself from the Democrats. The Whigs' only two successful presidential candidates (William Henry Harrison and Zachary Taylor) were popular military heroes who ran largely issueless campaigns for office. When the party ran General Winfield Scott, yet another military figure, for president in 1852 on a vague and uninspiring platform, support for the Whigs collapsed throughout the country.

The demise of the Whig Party unleashed a scramble to find new issues and establish new organizations around which politicians could mobilize voters. At first it appeared that the void might be filled by the anti-immigrant and anti-Catholic American Party, often referred to as the "Know Nothings." The American Party achieved significant success in the 1854 elections and seemed poised to become the chief political alternative to the Democrats. The passage of the Kansas-Nebraska Act that year, however, provided an opening for those northern politicians, organized in the newly established Republican Party, who preferred to mobilize voters around the issue of slavery's expansion. In the 1856 campaign, Republicans made effective use of the violence in Kansas and the caning of Massachusetts Senator Charles Sumner by South Carolina Congressman Preston Brooks to establish themselves as the dominant party in the North. Freed from any connection to southern politicians and interests, Republicans were able to strike a militant pose against the depredations of what they termed the "slave power." Northern Democrats, by contrast, were constrained by their need to placate their southern party mates and found themselves increasingly portrayed by Republicans as puppets and dupes of the "slave power."

The South witnessed a parallel development with militant pro-slavery politics increasingly filling the void left by the demise of the old party system. In 1850, a small group of extremist southern politicians known as "fire-eaters" had advocated secession if any restrictions whatsoever were applied to slave owners carrying their human property into the territories of the West. The South's established political leadership, though, was able to marginalize the fire-eaters, and a compromise solution to the slavery expansion issue was found. Over the course of the 1850s, the fire-eaters were nonetheless able to develop a significant following that threatened the South's traditional political leaders. Fire-eaters portrayed northern Republicans as a threat to slavery and warned southern voters, most of whom were not slave owners, that an end to the institution would undermine the status of all white people. More moderate southern politicians felt compelled to prove their "pro-southern" credentials; and the most effective way to do so was to stake out the most militant possible position on any and all real or perceived threats to southern interests and to the institution of slavery. Ironically, the hard-line stance adopted by mainstream Southern Democrats to fend off the fire-eaters undermined Northern Democrats and fostered the very rise of the Republican Party that Southern fire-eaters held up as evidence of a growing threat to slavery and to the South.

The sectional conflict over slavery was not irrepressible; but by 1860; it could no longer be repressed. The institutional links that had bound northern and southern politicians to each other had been severed. In their place was a political dynamic that encouraged politicians both North and South to play the role of sectional champion while, at all costs, avoiding any compromise that could be portrayed as a sectional sellout. As Michael Holt writes, "national elections came to be viewed by many as less a question of which party than of which section would control the government in Washington."[4] The election of Abraham Lincoln to the presidency in 1860 virtually required southern politicians, regardless of their personal sentiments, to initiate the process of secession for fear of appearing soft. Northern Republicans, by contrast, had little option but to stand fast against what they had long portrayed as the bullying political tactics of southerners. The American political system had lost the ability to contain the slavery controversy. The result—a result that few could have foreseen and even fewer desired—was the most destructive conflict in American History.

---

4   Holt, *Political Crisis,* 183.

DEBATING THE QUESTION

THE SECTIONAL CRISIS

Prior to the 1850s, political divisions within the United States fell primarily along party lines. National elections pitted two major parties (Whigs and the Democrats) against each other. Both parties were national in scope, with supporters throughout the country. The leaders of both parties worked to minimize the role of sectionally divisive issues in national political campaigns. In the 1850s, however, national politics rapidly polarized along lines of North versus South. The sectionally divisive question of the expansion of slavery into the western territories came to overshadow the issues that had previously divided Whigs and Democrats, and efforts to find a compromise solution to the slavery controversy ended in failure. In the early 1850s, the Whig Party collapsed, and the void it left was filled by the newly organized Republicans—a northern-based party dedicated to halting the expansion of slavery. As voters in the North flocked to the Republicans, the Democratic Party began to shed northern support and became increasingly dominated by southern slaveholding interests. In 1860, northern votes elected Republican candidate Abraham Lincoln to the presidency, a result that served as the spark for secession and war. Explaining why national politics polarized so rapidly along sectional lines of North versus South is necessary for answering the question of why civil war erupted in the United States in 1861.

1.1 FREDERICK DOUGLASS, "WHAT TO THE SLAVE IS THE FOURTH OF JULY" (1851) AND SALMON P. CHASE, ET AL., "APPEAL OF THE INDEPENDENT DEMOCRATS" (1854)

The late 1820s and 1830s saw the emergence in the North of an abolitionist movement dedicated to the full and complete eradication of the institution of slavery from the United States of America. Though this movement gained a significant following in the North, particularly among evangelical Protestants and African Americans, the call to immediately abolish slavery never commanded majority sentiment in the region prior to the Civil War. In the late 1840s and 1850s, by contrast, most did rally to the demand that the expansion of slavery into the new territories of the West be halted. The so-called free soil issue helped propel the newly established Republican Party to prominence in the North and fueled Abraham Lincoln's successful campaign for the presidency in 1860.

These two documents provide a contrast between the abolitionist and free soil positions. The first contains excerpts from a speech delivered by the famed African American abolitionist Frederick Douglass in 1852. Douglass was born into slavery in the state of Maryland and as a young man escaped north to freedom where he became active on the movement to abolish slavery. The second document is an 1854 appeal issued by a group of northern congressmen against the proposed Kansas-Nebraska Act, which would open the territories of the Great Plains to slavery. As you read the documents, look for ways in which the abolitionist and free soil positions differ.

GUIDING QUESTIONS:

1. On what basis does Douglass critique the institution of slavery? What reasons does he give his audience to oppose the institution of slavery?
2. On what basis does the "Appeal" criticize the expansion of slavery? What reasons do the authors give their readers to oppose slavery's expansion?
3. How do the anti-slavery arguments of Douglass and the "Appeal" differ from each other?

WHAT TO THE SLAVE IS THE FOURTH OF JULY?

FREDERICK DOUGLASS, JULY 5, 1852

MEETING SPONSORED BY THE ROCHESTER LADIES' ANTI-SLAVERY SOCIETY, ROCHESTER HALL, ROCHESTER, N.Y.

Fellow-citizens, pardon me, allow me to ask, . . . why am I called upon to speak here to-day? What have I, or those I represent, to do with your national independence? Are the great principles of political freedom and of natural justice, embodied in that Declaration of Independence, extended to us? and am I, therefore, called upon to bring our humble offering to the national altar, and to confess the benefits and express devout gratitude for the blessings resulting from your independence to us?

Would to God, both for your sakes and ours, that an affirmative answer could be truthfully returned to these questions! Then would my task be light, and my burden easy and delightful. For who is there so cold, that a nation's sympathy could not warm him? Who so obdurate and dead to the claims of gratitude, that would not thankfully acknowledge such priceless benefits? Who so stolid and selfish, that would not give his voice to swell the hallelujahs of a nation's jubilee, when the chains of servitude had been torn from his limbs? I am not that man. In a case like that, the dumb might eloquently speak, and the "lame man leap as an hart."

But, such is not the state of the case. I say it with a sad sense of the disparity between us. I am not included within the pale of this glorious anniversary! Your high independence only reveals the immeasurable distance between us. The blessings in which you, this day, rejoice, are not enjoyed in common. The rich inheritance of justice, liberty, prosperity and independence, bequeathed by your fathers, is shared by you, not by me. The sunlight that brought life and healing to you, has brought stripes and death to me. This Fourth [of] July is yours, not mine. You may rejoice, I must mourn. To drag a man in fetters into the grand illuminated temple of liberty, and call upon him to join you in joyous anthems, were inhuman mockery and sacrilegious irony. Do you mean, citizens, to mock me, by asking me to speak to-day? If so, there is a parallel to your conduct. And let me warn you that it is dangerous to copy the example of a nation whose crimes, lowering up to heaven, were thrown down by the breath of the Almighty, burying that nation in irrecoverable ruin! I can to-day take up the plaintive lament of a peeled and woe-smitten people!

"By the rivers of Babylon, there we sat down. Yea! we wept when we remembered Zion. We hanged our harps upon the willows in the midst thereof. For there, they that carried us away captive, required of us a song; and they who wasted us required of us mirth, saying, Sing us one of the songs of Zion. How can we sing the Lord's song in a strange land? If I forget thee, O Jerusalem, let my right hand forget her cunning. If I do not remember thee, let my tongue cleave to the roof of my mouth."

Fellow-citizens; above your national, tumultuous joy, I hear the mournful wail of millions! whose chains, heavy and grievous yesterday, are, to-day, rendered more intolerable by the jubilee shouts that reach them. If I do forget, if I do not faithfully remember those bleeding children of sorrow this day, "may my right hand forget her cunning, and may my tongue cleave to the roof of my mouth!" To forget them, to pass lightly over their wrongs, and to chime in with the popular theme, would be treason most scandalous and shocking, and would make me a reproach before God and the world. My subject, then fellow-citizens, is AMERICAN SLAVERY. I shall see, this day, and its popular characteristics, from the slave's point of view. Standing, there, identified with the American bondman, making his wrongs mine, I do not hesitate to declare, with all my soul, that the character and conduct of this nation never looked blacker to me than on this 4th of July! Whether we turn to the declarations of the past, or to the professions of the present, the conduct of the nation seems equally hideous and revolting. America is false to the past, false to the present, and solemnly binds herself to be false to the future. Standing with God and the crushed and bleeding slave on this occasion, I will, in the name of humanity which is outraged, in the name of liberty which is fettered, in the name of the constitution and the Bible, which are disregarded and trampled upon, dare to call in question and to denounce, with all the emphasis I can command, everything that serves to perpetuate slavery-the great sin and shame of America! "I will not equivocate; I will not excuse;" I will use the severest language I can command; and yet not one word shall escape me that any man, whose judgment is not blinded by prejudice, or who is not at heart a slaveholder, shall not confess to be right and just.

But I fancy I hear some one of my audience say, it is just in this circumstance that you and your brother abolitionists fail to make a favorable impression on the public mind. Would you argue more, and denounce less, would you persuade more, and rebuke less, your cause would be much more likely to succeed. But, I submit, where all is plain there is nothing to be argued. What point in the anti-slavery creed would you have me argue? On what branch of the subject do the people of this country need light? Must I undertake to prove that the slave is a man?

That point is conceded already. Nobody doubts it. The slaveholders themselves acknowledge it in the enactment of laws for their government. They acknowledge it when they punish disobedience on the part of the slave. There are seventy-two crimes in the State of Virginia, which, if committed by a black man, (no matter how ignorant he be), subject him to the punishment of death; while only two of the same crimes will subject a white man to the like punishment. What is this but the acknowledgement that the slave is a moral, intellectual and responsible being? The manhood of the slave is conceded. It is admitted in the fact that Southern statute books are covered with enactments forbidding, under severe fines and penalties, the teaching of the slave to read or to write. When you can point to any such laws, in reference to the beasts of the field, then I may consent to argue the manhood of the slave. When the dogs in your streets, when the fowls of the air, when the cattle on your hills, when the fish of the sea, and the reptiles that crawl, shall be unable to distinguish the slave from a brute, then will I argue with you that the slave is a man!

For the present, it is enough to affirm the equal manhood of the Negro race. Is it not astonishing that, while we are ploughing, planting and reaping, using all kinds of mechanical tools, erecting houses, constructing bridges, building ships, working in metals of brass, iron, copper, silver and gold; that, while we are reading, writing and cyphering, acting as clerks, merchants and secretaries, having among us lawyers, doctors, ministers, poets, authors, editors, orators and teachers; that, while we are engaged in all manner of enterprises common to other men, digging gold in California, capturing the whale in the Pacific, feeding sheep and cattle on the hill-side, living, moving, acting, thinking, planning, living in families as husbands, wives and children, and, above all, confessing and worshipping the Christian's God, and looking hopefully for life and immortality beyond the grave, we are called upon to prove that we are men!

Would you have me argue that man is entitled to liberty? that he is the rightful owner of his own body? You have already declared it. Must I argue the wrongfulness of slavery? Is that a question for Republicans? Is it to be settled by the rules of logic and argumentation, as a matter beset with great difficulty, involving a doubtful

application of the principle of justice, hard to be understood? How should I look to-day, in the presence of Americans, dividing, and subdividing a discourse, to show that men have a natural right to freedom? speaking of it relatively, and positively, negatively, and affirmatively. To do so, would be to make myself ridiculous, and to offer an insult to your understanding. There is not a man beneath the canopy of heaven, that does not know that slavery is wrong for him.

What, am I to argue that it is wrong to make men brutes, to rob them of their liberty, to work them without wages, to keep them ignorant of their relations to their fellow men, to beat them with sticks, to flay their flesh with the lash, to load their limbs with irons, to hunt them with dogs, to sell them at auction, to sunder their families, to knock out their teeth, to burn their flesh, to starve them into obedience and submission to their masters? Must I argue that a system thus marked with blood, and stained with pollution, is wrong? No! I will not. I have better employments for my time and strength than such arguments would imply.

What, then, remains to be argued? Is it that slavery is not divine; that God did not establish it; that our doctors of divinity are mistaken? There is blasphemy in the thought. That which is inhuman, cannot be divine! Who can reason on such a proposition? They that can, may; I cannot. The time for such argument is past.

At a time like this, scorching irony, not convincing argument, is needed. O! had I the ability, and could I reach the nation's ear, I would, to-day, pour out a fiery stream of biting ridicule, blasting reproach, withering sarcasm, and stern rebuke. For it is not light that is needed, but fire; it is not the gentle shower, but thunder. We need the storm, the whirlwind, and the earthquake. The feeling of the nation must be quickened; the conscience of the nation must be roused; the propriety of the nation must be startled; the hypocrisy of the nation must be exposed; and its crimes against God and man must be proclaimed and denounced.

What, to the American slave, is your 4th of July? I answer: a day that reveals to him, more than all other days in the year, the gross injustice and cruelty to which he is the constant victim. To him, your celebration is a sham; your boasted liberty, an unholy license; your national greatness, swelling vanity; your sounds of rejoicing are empty and heartless; your denunciations of tyrants, brass fronted impudence; your shouts of liberty and equality, hollow mockery; your prayers and hymns, your sermons and thanksgivings, with all your religious parade, and solemnity, are, to him, mere bombast, fraud, deception, impiety, and hypocrisy—a thin veil to cover up crimes which would disgrace a nation of savages. There is not a nation on the earth guilty of practices, more shocking and bloody, than are the people of these United States, at this very hour.

Go where you may, search where you will, roam through all the monarchies and despotisms of the old world, travel through South America, search out every abuse, and when you have found the last, lay your facts by the side of the everyday practices of this nation, and you will say with me, that, for revolting barbarity and shameless hypocrisy, America reigns without a rival. . . .

APPEAL OF THE INDEPENDENT DEMOCRATS IN CONGRESS, TO THE PEOPLE OF THE UNITED STATES. SHALL SLAVERY BE PERMITTED IN NEBRASKA? WASHINGTON, JANUARY 19, 1854.

FELLOW-CITIZENS: As Senators and Representatives in the Congress of the United States, it is our duty to warn our constituents whenever imminent danger menaces the freedom of our institutions or the permanency of our Union.

Such danger, as we firmly believe, now impends, and we earnestly solicit your prompt attention to it.

At the last session of Congress, a bill for the organization of the Territory of Nebraska passed the House of Representatives with an overwhelming majority. That bill was based on the principle of excluding slavery from the new Territory. It was not taken up for consideration in the Senate, and consequently failed to become a law.

At the present session a new Nebraska bill has been reported by the Senate Committee on Territories, which, should it unhappily receive the sanction of Congress, will open all the unorganized territory of the Union to the ingress of slavery.

We arraign this bill as a gross violation of a sacred pledge; as a criminal betrayal of precious rights; as part and parcel of an atrocious plot to exclude from a vast unoccupied region, immigrants from the Old World and free laborers from our own States, and convert it into a dreary region of despotism, inhabited by masters and slaves.

Take your maps, fellowcitizens, we entreat you, and see what country it is which this bill, gratuitously and recklessly, proposes to open to slavery.

From the southwestern corner of Missouri pursue the parallel of 36 deg. 30 min. north latitude, westerly across the Arkansas, across the north fork of Canadian, to the northeastern angle of Texas; then following the northern boundary or Texas to the western limit of New Mexico; then proceed along that western line to its northern termination; then again turn westwardly and follow the northern line of New Mexico to the crest of the Rocky Mountains; then ascend northwardly along the crest of that mountain range to the line which separates the United States from the British possessions in North America, on the 49th parallel of north latitude; then pursue your course eastwardly along that line to the White Earth river, which falls into the Missouri from the north; descend that river to its confluence with the Missouri; descend the Missouri, along the western border of Minnesota, of Iowa, of Missouri, to the point where it ceases to be a boundary line, and enters the State to which it gives its name; then continue your southward course along the western limit of that State to the point from which you set out. You have now made the circuit of the proposed Territory of Nebraska. You have traversed the vast distance of more than three thousand miles. You have traced the outline of an area of four hundred and eighty-five thousand square miles; more than twelve times as great as that of Ohio.

This immense region, occupying the very heart of the North American continent, and larger, by thirty-three thousand square miles, than all the existing free States, excluding California—this immense region, well watered and fertile, through which the middle and northern routes from the Atlantic to the Pacific must pass—this immense region, embracing all the unorganized territory of the nation, except the comparatively insignificant district of Indian territory north of Red river and between Arkansas and Texas, and now for more than thirty years regarded by the common consent of the American people as consecrated to freedom, by statute and by compact—this immense region, the bill now before the Senate, without reason and without excuse, but in flagrant disregard of sound policy and sacred faith, proposes open to slavery.

We beg your attention, fellow-citizens, to a few historical facts.

The original settled policy of the United States, clearly indicated by the Jefferson proviso of 1784, and by the ordinance of 1787, was non-extension of slavery.

In 1803, Louisiana was acquired by purchase from France. At that time there were borne twenty-five or thirty thousand slaves in this Territory, most of them within what is now the State of Louisiana; a few, only, further north, on the west bank of the Mississippi. Congress, instead of providing for the abolition of slavery in this new Territory, permitted its continuance. In 1812 the State of Louisiana was organized and admitted into the Union with slavery.

In 1818, six years later, the inhabitants of the Territory of Missouri applied to Congress for authority to form a State constitution, and for admission into the Union. There were, at that time, in the whole territory acquired from France, outside of the State of Louisiana, not three thousand slaves.

There was no apology in the circumstances of the country for the continuance of slavery. The original national policy was against it, and, not less, the plain language of the treaty under which the territory had been acquired from France.

It was proposed, therefore, to incorporate in the bill authorizing the formation of a State Government, a provision requiring that the constitution of the new State should contain an article providing for the abolition of existing slavery, and prohibiting the further introduction of slaves.

This provision was vehemently and pertinaciously opposed; but finally prevailed in the House of Representatives by a decided vote. In the Senate it was rejected, and, in consequence of the disagreement between the two Houses, the bill was lost.

At the next session of Congress the controversy was renewed with increased violence. It was terminated, at length, by a compromise. Missouri was allowed to come into the Union with slavery, but a section was inserted in the act authorizing her admission, excluding slavery, forever, from all the territory acquired from France, not included in the new State, lying north of 36 deg. 30 min.

We quote the prohibitory section:

"SEC 8. *Be it further enacted,* That in all that territory ceded by France to the United States, under the name Louisiana, which lies north of thirty-six degrees and thirty minutes of north latitude, not included within the limits of the State contemplated by this act, slavery and involuntary servitude, otherwise than as the punishment of crimes, shall be and is hereby forever prohibited."

The question of the constitutionality of this prohibition was submitted by President Monroe to his cabinet. John Quincy Adams was then Secretary of State; John C. Calhoun was Secretary of War; William H. Crawford was Secretary of the Treasury; and William Wirt was Attorney General. Each of these eminent men, three of them being from slave States, gave a written opinion, affirming its constitutionality, and thereupon the act received the sanction of the President himself, also from a slave State.

Nothing is more certain in history than the fact, that Missouri could not have been admitted as a slave State had not certain members from the free States been reconciled to the measure by the incorporation of this prohibition into the act of admission. Nothing is more certain than that this prohibition has been regarded and accepted by the whole country as a solemn compact against the extension of slavery into any part of the territory acquired from France, lying north of 36 deg. 30 min., and not included in the new State of Missouri. The same act—let it be ever remembered—which authorized the formation of a constitution for the State, without a clause forbidding slavery, consecrated, beyond question and beyond honest recall, the whole remainder of the territory to freedom and free institutions forever. For more than thirty years—during more than half the period of our national existence under our present constitution—this compact has been universally regarded and acted upon as inviolable American law. In conformity with it, Iowa was admitted as a free State, and Minnesota has been organized as a free Territory.

It is a strange and ominous fact, well calculated to awaken the worst apprehensions, and the most fearful forebodings of future calamities, that it is now deliberately purposed to repeal this prohibition, by implication or directly—the latter certainly the manlier way—and thus to subvert this compact, and allow slavery in all the yet unorganized territory.

We cannot, in this address, review the various pretences [*sic*] under which it is attempted to cloak this monstrous wrong; but we must not altogether omit to notice one.

It is said that the Territory of Nebraska sustains the same relations to slavery as did the territory acquired from Mexico prior to 1850, and that the pro-slavery clauses of the bill are necessary to carry into effect the compromises of that year.

No assertion could be more groundless.

Three acquisitions of territory have been made by treaty. The first was from France. Out of this territory have been created the three slave States of Louisiana, Arkansas, Missouri, and the single free State of Iowa. The controversy which arose in relation to the then unorganized portion of this territory was closed in 1820, by the Missouri act, containing the slavery prohibition, as has been already stated. This controversy related only to territory acquired from France. The act, by which it was terminated, was confined, by its own express terms, to the same territory, and had no relation to any other.

The second acquisition was from Spain. Florida, the territory thus acquired, was yielded to slavery without a struggle, and almost without a murmur.

The third was from Mexico. The controversy which arose from this acquisition is fresh in the re-membrance of the American people. Out of it sprung the acts of Congress, commonly known as the compromise measures of 1850, by one of which California was admitted as a free State; while two others, organizing the Territories of New Mexico and Utah, exposed all the residue of the recently acquired territory to the invasion of slavery.

These acts were never supposed to abrogate or touch the existing exclusion of slavery from what is now called Nebraska. They applied to the territory acquired from Mexico, and to that only. They were intended as a settlement of the controversy growing out of that acquisition, and of that controversy only. They must stand or fall by their own merits.

The statesmen whose powerful support carried the Utah and New Mexico acts, never dreamed that their provisions would ever be applied to Nebraska. Even at the last session of Congress, Mr. Atchison, of Missouri, in a speech in favor of taking up the former Nebraska bill, on the morning of the 4th of March, 1853, said: "It is evident that the Missouri Compromise cannot be repealed. So far as that question is concerned, we might as well agree to the admission of this Territory now, as next year, or five or ten years hence." Those words could not have fallen from this watchful guardian of slavery had he supposed that this territory was embraced by the pro-slavery provisions of the compromise acts. This pretension had not then been set up. It is a palpable after-thought.

The compromise acts themselves refute this pretension. In the third article of the second section of the joint resolution for annexing Texas to the United States, it is expressly declared that "in such State or States as shall be formed out of said territory north of said Missouri compromise line, slavery or involuntary servitude, except for crime, shall be prohibited;" and in the act for organizing New Mexico and settling the boundary of Texas, a proviso was incorporated, on the motion of Mr. Mason, of Virginia, which distinctly preserves this prohibition, and flouts the bare-faced pretension that all the territory of the United States, whether south or north of the Missouri compromise line, is to be open to slavery. It is as follows:

"*Provided*, That nothing herein contained shall be construed to impair or qualify anything contained in the third article of the second section of the joint Resolution for annexing Texas to the United States, approved March 1, 1845, either as regards the number of States that may hereafter be formed out of the State of Texas or otherwise."

Here is proof, beyond controversy, that the principle of the Missouri act prohibiting slavery north of 36 deg. 30 min., far from being abrogated by the compromise acts, is expressly affirmed; and that the proposed repeal of this prohibition, instead of being an affirmation of the compromise acts, is a repeal of a very prominent provision of the most important act of the series. It is solemnly declared in the very compromise acts "that *nothing herein contained shall be construed to impair or qualify*" the prohibition of slavery north of 36 deg. 30 min., and yet, in the face of this declaration, that sacred prohibition is said to be overthrown. Can presumption further go? To all who, in any way, lean upon these compromises, we commend this exposition.

The pretences, therefore, that the territory, covered by the positive prohibition of 1820, sustains a similar relation to slavery with that acquired from Mexico, covered by no prohibition except that of disputed constitutional or Mexican law, and that the compromises of 1850 require the incorporation of the proslavery causes of the Utah and New Mexico bill in the Nebraska act, are mere inventions, designed to cover up from public reprehension meditated bad faith. Were he living now, no one would be more forward, more eloquent, or more indignant, in his denunciation of that bad faith, than Henry Clay, the foremost champion of both compromises.

In 1820 the slave States said to the free States: "Admit Missouri with slavery and refrain from positive exclusion south of 36 deg. 30 min., and we will join you in perpetual prohibition north of that line." The free States consented. In 1854 the slave States say to the free States, "Missouri is admitted; no prohibition of slavery south of 36 deg. 30 min. has been attempted; we have received the full consideration of our agreement; no more is to be gained by adherence to it on our part; we, therefore, propose to cancel the compact." If this be not Punic faith, what is it? Not without the deepest dishonor and crime can the free States acquiesce in this demand.

We confess our total inability properly to delineate the character or describe the consequences of this measure. Language fails to express the sentiments of indignation and abhorrence which it inspires; and no vision, less penetrating and comprehensive than that of the All-Seeing, can reach its evil issues.

To some of its more immediate and inevitable consequences, however, we must attempt to direct your attention.

What will be the effect of this measure, should it unhappily become a law, upon the proposed Pacific railroad? We have already said that two of the principal routes, the central and the northern, traverse this territory. If slavery be allowed there, the settlement and cultivation of the country must be greatly retarded. Inducements to the immigration of free laborers will be almost destroyed. The enhanced cost of construction, and the diminished expectation of profitable returns, will present almost insuperable obstacles to building the rood at all; while, even if made, the difficulty and expense of keeping it up, in a country from which the energetic and intelligent masses will be virtually excluded, will greatly impair its usefulness and value.

From the rich lands of this large Territory also, patriotic statesmen have anticipated that a free, industrious, and enlightened population will extract abundant treasures of individual and public wealth. There, it has been expected, freedom-loving emigrants from Europe, and energetic and intelligent laborers from our own land, will find homes of comfort and fields of enterprise. If this bill shall become a law, all such expectation will tum to grievous disappointment. The blight of slavery will cover the land. The homestead law, should Congress enact one, will be worthless there. Freemen, unless pressed by a hard and cruel necessity, will not, and should not, work beside slaves. Labor cannot be respected where any class of laborer is held in abject bondage.

We earnestly request the enlightened conductors of newspapers printed in the German and other foreign languages to direct the attention of their readers to this important matter.

It is of immense consequence, also, to scrutinize the geographical character of this project. We beg you, fellow-citizens, to observe that it will sever the east from the west of the United States by a wide slave-holding belt of country, extending from the Gulf of Mexico to British North America. It is a bold scheme against American liberty, worthy of an accomplished architect of ruin. Texas is already slaveholding, and occupies the Gulf region from the Sabine to the Rio Grande, and from the Gulf of Mexico to the Red river. North of the Red river, and extending between Texas and Arkansas, to the parallel of 36 deg. 30 min., lies the Indian territory, about equal in extent to the latter State, in which slavery was not prohibited by the act of 1820. From 36 deg. 30 min. to the boundary line between our own country and the British possessions, stretching from west to east through more than eleven degrees longitude, and from south to north through more than twelve degrees of latitude, extends the great territory, the fate of which is now to be determined by the American Congress. Thus you see, fellow-citizens, that the first operation of the proposed permission of slavery in Nebraska, will be to stay the progress of the free States westward, and to cut off the free States of the Pacific from the free States of the Atlantic. It is hoped, doubtless, by compelling the whole commerce and the whole travel between the east and the west to pass for hundreds of miles through a slaveholding region, in the heart of the continent, and by the influence of a Federal Government controlled by the slave power, we extinguish and establish slavery in the States and Territories of the Pacific, and thus permanently subjugate the whole country to the yoke of a slaveholding despotism. Shall a plot against humanity and democracy, so monstrous, and so dangerous to the interests of liberty throughout the world, be permitted to succeed?

We appeal to the People. We warn you that the dearest interests of freedom and the Union are in imminent peril. Demagogues may tell you that the Union can be maintained only by submitting to the demands of slavery. We tell you that the safety of the Union can only be insured by the full recognition of the just claims of freedom and man. The Union was formed to establish justice, and secure the blessings of liberty. When it fails to accomplish these ends it will be worthless, and when it becomes worthless it cannot long endure.

We entreat you to be mindful of that fundamental maxim of democracy, EQUAL RIGHTS AND EXACT JUSTICE FOR ALL MEN. Do not submit to become agents in extending legalized oppression and systematic injustice over a vast territory yet exempt from these terrible evils.

We implore Christians and Christian ministers to interpose. Their divine religion requires them to behold in every man a brother, and to labor for the advancement and regeneration of the human race.

Whatever apologies may be offered for the toleration of slavery in the States, none can be urged for its extension into Territories where it does not exist, and where that extension involves the repeal of ancient law, and the violation of solemn compact. Let all protest, earnestly and emphatically, by correspondence, through the press, by memorials, by resolutions of public meetings and legislative bodies, and in whatever other mode may seem expedient, against this enormous crime.

For ourselves, we shall resist it by speech and vote, and with all the abilities which God has given us. Even if overcome in the impending struggle, we shall not submit. We shall go home to our constituents; erect anew the standard of freedom, and call on the people to come to the rescue of the country from the domination of slavery. We will not despair: for the cause of human freedom is the cause of God.

S. P. CHASE, *Senator from Ohio.*
CHARLES SUMNER, *Senator from Mass.*
J. R. GIDDINGS, *Representative from Ohio.*
EDWARD WADE, *Representative from Ohio.*
GERRITT SMITH, *Representative from New York.*
ALEX. DE WITT, *Representative from Mass.*

DRAWING CONCLUSIONS:

1. What can we learn from these documents about free soil politics and how it differed from abolitionism? Why did the free soil position gain a broader following than did abolitionism?
2. What else can we learn about the political views of northerners from these documents?

1.2 SPEECHES OF SENATOR ALBERT G. BROWN (1859) AND REPRESENTATIVE LUCIUS GARTRELL (1860)

The 1850s also saw the growth of what came to be known as "southern rights" sentiment. Southern rights advocates argued that discrimination against slave property was an assault on the rights of southerners. Spokespersons for southern rights demanded that slave owners be allowed to take their slave property into the new territories of the west and that fugitive slaves who had escaped north be returned to their masters, as required by the US Constitution. These two documents provide examples of southern rights sentiment. Both are speeches delivered to the US Congress by southern members. The first is from Senator Albert G. Brown of Mississippi. The second is from Representative Lucius Jeremiah Gartrell of Georgia.

GUIDING QUESTIONS:

1. In what ways exactly do Senator Brown and Representative Gartrell say northerners have attacked the rights of southerners?
2. How would you describe the emotional content of the speeches? How do Brown and Gartrell *feel* about northerners and the things they accuse them of doing to southerners?

SPEECH OF SENATOR ALBERT G. BROWN (DEMOCRAT-MISSISSIPPI) TO THE US SENATE, DECEMBER 19, 1859

MR. BROWN. You did not go to war for that; but I noticed that you went to war when other people's rights were invaded. I state the fact, that during the administration of Martin Van Buren, a cargo of slaves sailed from Alexandria, and by stress of weather were driven into St. Thomas, and set free by the British Government, and reparation has never been made. My friends say it was the Bahamas. It does not matter where they were driven; reparation has never been made. If it had been a cargo of live stock, who does not know that, if a question had been raised, the Government would have never ceased negotiations. If it had been a cargo of dry goods or New England rum that had been confiscated, who does not know that this Government never would have ceased until it had got reparation.

All we ask—and, in asking that, we shall never cease—is, that our property, under the common Government, be put upon the same footing with other people's property; that this Government of ours shall be allowed to draw no insulting discrimination between slave property and any other kind of property; that wherever the authority of the Government extends, it shall be given to us in an equal degree with anybody else; and, by that, I say again, I mean given to the extent of affording us adequate and sufficient protection. Who does not know that, in the last two or three years, emigrant trains were robbed in Utah by the Mormons; not robbed of slaves, but robbed of other kinds of property. What was done? An army was promptly sent to repair the injury, at an expense, I dare say, when we shall sum up the bill and pay it, of $20,000,000. Who believes that if the property had been our slaves, any reparation would have been insisted upon? Is the Government so prompt to send

From *Congressional Globe*, 36th Cong, 1st Sess, p. 393.

armies to protect us against the underground process? No. Twenty millions of property may be stolen from us, and the Government stands by and contents itself with simply remonstrating, with giving gentle hints that it is all wrong. When I say this is done by the Government, I do not mean the Government of James Buchanan, or Franklin Pierce, or Millard Fillmore; but I mean the Government in whosoever hands it happened to rest. Justice has never been done us; our property has never been treated like the property of other people; has never received the same sort of protection, the same kind of security. While the Government has been ready to protect other people's property on the high seas and in the Territories; while it has been ready to make war at home and declare war against foreign countries for the protection of other people's property, we have received no such guarantees from it. I demand them. I demand to be treated as an equal. If you will insist upon taxing me as an equal, I do not feel disposed to come up and pay my taxes, simply to know the Government through its power to make exactions on me. I do not choose to perform military service, and spill my blood and risk my life and lay down the lives of my people for the common protection, in defense of a Government which only knows me through its powers to tax me. I claim the same right to protection on the part of my people as I concede to you. Wherever your property is on the face of God's habitable globe, on the sea or on the land, I claim that the arms and power of this Government must go to protect and defend it. For that was the great object of creating the Government; and when it falls short of that object, it fails in its great mission, the great purpose for which it was created.

I know of no mission which this Government has to perform except to protect the citizen in his life, his liberty, and his property. When it fails in these great essentials, it has failed in everything; and I stand even in this august presence to say, as I have said in the more august presence of my immediate constituents, the Legislature of my State—and if they choose to repudiate me for saying it, I am willing to be repudiated—that whenever the Government fails, I do not ask it to refuse, but when it fails to protect me and my people in our lives, our liberties, and our property, upon the high seas or upon the land, it ought to

be abolished. If that be treason, gentlemen, make the most of it. That is all I have said; and by that proposition living or dying, sinking or swimming, surviving or perishing, I mean to stand here and elsewhere.

Those who have served with me in this House and in the other House of Congress, know, or ought to know, that I am deeply and earnestly and at heart devoted to the Democratic party. I am devoted to it, because I have always regarded it as a party that dispensed equal and exact justice to every part of the country. I am a Democrat because I have always felt that this Government would dispense to Massachusetts the same measure of justice that it gave to Mississippi; that it would give to Pennsylvania no more than it gave to Virginia; and I should be as ready to despise it if I thought it would give more to my State than to any other State in the Confederacy. While I say this, I am equally free to say, that I would, if it were in my power, rend it into ten thousand fragments, if it exacted of me to do that for Massachusetts which the Senator from Massachusetts would not do for Mississippi. If I have asked, in all this, anything more for my country, for my State, or for my section, than I would give to any other State or section, show me in what, and I am ready to submit. I ask nothing for my section that I am not willing to yield to any other.

Now, Mr. President, thanking the Republican benches for the patient and polite attention which they have given me, I take my seat. [Laughter, every seat on the Republican side being vacant.]

SPEECH OF REPRESENTATIVE LUCIUS JEREMIAH GARTRELL (DEMOCRAT-GEORGIA) TO THE HOUSE OF REPRESENTATIVES JANUARY 10, 1860

I was commenting, when interrupted, upon the remark of the gentleman from Pennsylvania that the North could manufacture more arms and ammunition than the South could buy. When they come down to the South, let me tell them, that we will be prepared to receive them, that every plowshare will be turned into a sword, and every plow-boy will stand ready to drive back the northern mercenaries. [Applause in the galleries.] Even the slaves will be ready to meet you, and defend the homes and firesides of their masters and mistresses. They would repulse you, for they scorn your interference in their behalf. They scout your abolitionism, your fanatics who neglect the poorer classes at your own homes. They say that you had better attend to your own paupers. Let me say to the gentleman from Ohio [Mr. STANTON] that I will take him to Georgia, if he pleases, and that if he finds a pauper negro there, I will give him ten for every one he finds. You never knew, sir, of a negro begging in the South; but go to the northern States, and see there the thousand emaciated hands stretched out for alms.

You talk about philanthropy and humanity! Attend to your own poor and your own affairs. "Physician, heal thyself." I do not allude to these things in any spirit of boasting. God knows I pity the poor men and the poor women of the northern States. I would have them come to the South, where there is a more genial climate, and where they could be fed, clothed, and protected, and nursed, when sick, by our slaves.

Gentlemen of the House, I thank you for your kind attention, and will detain you but a moment longer. A few days ago, the citizens of Savannah, a large commercial city of my State, observant of these insults and aggressions, met, as I am informed, without respect of party, and organized a vigilant association for the protection of the rights of themselves and their fellow-citizens. Among other things, they adopted some resolutions; which so fully coincide with my own opinions upon the present condition of the country, that I send them to the Clerk's desk and ask they may be read for the information of this House and the country.

The resolutions were read, as follows:

"4. *Resolved* That, looking forward to a time when all ties which now connect us with the northern States of this Confederacy may be severed, and considering that prudence as well as a proper regard for the interests of our own section demand that all our domestic resources should be fostered and developed, we earnestly recommend: 1. Direct foreign trade. 2. The patronage of southern commerce and manufactures. 3. Education in southern schools and colleges. 4. Patronage to southern authors and editors. 5. The employment of southern teachers, and the use of southern school books. 6. Non-intercourse with all cities and sections at the North inimical to slavery and southern institutions. And to secure respect to these recommendations, we individually and collectively pledge ourselves in all cases to prefer in our business, or for our use, the natural and artificial productions of the South to all others, and goods of foreign origin which have been imported *directly* into a southern port, to those of the same character imported through a northern port.

"5. *Resolved*, That we earnestly request of the various transportation lines of this and the adjacent States, that they will so modify their rates of freight that the iron, coal, slate, granite, lime and other mineral productions of our own and the adjoining States, may be brought to this market at prices which will enable them to compete with similar articles of northern production.

"6. *Resolved*, That we recommend to our Legislature, 1. To establish a normal school, at which teachers may be trained, who shall, in all cases, be preferred as instructors in the free schools of this State. 2. To require that all the books used in the free schools of this State shall be the productions of southern authors, and be printed on southern paper by southern presses.

"7. *Resolved*, That we recommend to those of our citizens who have habitually, during their annual visits to the North, and at other times, purchased their supplies of dry goods, groceries, hardware, and other articles from northern merchants, hereafter to extend their patronage in these respects to the dealers in such commodities who are part of our own people, share in the defense of our institutions, and contribute to our prosperity.

"8. *Resolved*, That African slavery, as it exists in these United States, is morally and politically right, and is a blessing to both races, and the world at large; and that it is our duty, as patriots and Christians, to expand and perpetuate it.

"9. *Resolved*, That we ask no guarantee for the institution of slavery, founded, as it is, in the natural conditions of man, and established by divine appointment. We only demand that it shall be left alone, to stand or fall upon its own merits. But inasmuch as the rendition of fugitive slaves was a condition precedent to the formation and adoption of the Federal Constitution, it is incumbent and obligatory upon the General Government, and upon each of the

State governments, to adopt and enforce such measures as will effectually carry out a constitutional provision so just and so indispensable. We consider, therefore, that such States as have passed laws in opposition to this provision of the Constitution, with intent to hinder, prevent, or render difficult the speedy rendition of fugitive slaves, have violated the original compact of the Union between the States, and that they are in open rebellion to the General Government, and, as a consequence, are not entitled to representation in the Halls of Congress. Therefore, we recommend to our Senators and Representatives in Congress to object, in the most effectual manner in their power, to the admission into their respective Houses of Representatives from any and all such rebellious and revolutionary States."

MR. GARTRELL. Those resolutions speak for themselves, and I shall attempt no comment upon them, more than to call upon gentlemen from the North to note the fact that our people are not laboring under such a delusion us you suppose; that they are aroused to a keen sense of their rights, and will assert them fearlessly, and defend them at every hazard. Yet, we love the Union for its past glories; we desire that it may be perpetuated, and will never consent to violate the common Constitution of our fathers. You have placed your sacrilegious hands upon it, but southern men never will; and whenever your violations of it become too intolerable to be borne, I announce it now, in conclusion; us I did in the beginning that, although a love of Union animates our people, yet every man—yea, every matron and every fair daughter of the South—will exclaim with me, "Give us disunion rather than dishonor and disgrace." I thank the House for its patient attention and now yield the floor.

DRAWING CONCLUSION:

1. What can we learn from these documents about both the content of and the motivations behind the "southern rights" position?

1.3 SENATOR STEPHEN A. DOUGLAS TO THE EDITOR OF THE CONCORD (NEW HAMPSHIRE) *STATE CAPITAL REPORTER* (1854)

As politics polarized between the free soil position advocated by northern Republicans and the southern rights position taken by many in the South, a group of northern Democrats led by Senator Stephen Douglas of Illinois sought a middle ground. Douglass and his allies argued that the federal government should remain neutral on the issue of whether slavery should be allowed in the territories of the West and that instead the white settlers of each territory should make the decision for themselves. Douglass referred to this approach to the slavery extension question as "popular sovereignty." In this letter to a New Hampshire newspaper editor, Douglass responds to critics of popular sovereignty. Douglass had recently introduced the Kansas-Nebraska Act, which among other provisions applied the principle of popular sovereignty to western territories from which slavery had previously been banned; and he had come under withering criticism from those who argued that he had sold out to southern slaveholding interests. In this letter, Douglas defends the Kansas-Nebraska Act and the principle of popular sovereignty.

GUIDING QUESTIONS:

1. On what fundamental principle does Douglas say the concept of "popular sovereignty" rests?
2. What is Douglas' response to those who claim he had sold out to southern slaveholding interests?

STEPHEN DOUGLAS TO THE EDITOR OF THE CONCORD (NEW HAMPSHIRE) STATE CAPITAL REPORTER, FEBRUARY 16, 1854

WASHINGTON, *February 16, 1854*

SIR:

I am under obligation to you for your paper which has come to hand regularly from the commencement of the session. I saw with pleasure that you took a bold stand in favor of the Nebraska bill, and spoke in favorable terms of my speech in its support. In this you did no more than what might have been reasonably expected from a sound democratic paper. The bill rests upon, and proposes to carry into effect, the great fundamental principle of self-government upon which our republic institutions are predicated. It does not propose to legislate slavery into the Territories, nor out of the Territories. It does not propose to establish institutions for the people, nor to deprive them of the right of determining for themselves what kind of domestic institutions they may have. It presupposes that the people of the Territories are as intelligent, as wise, as patriotic, as conscientious as their brethren and kindred whom they left behind them in the States, and as they were before they emigrated to the Territories. By creating a territorial government we acknowledge that the people of the Territory ought to be erected into a distinct political organization. By giving them a territorial legislature, we acknowledge their capacity to legislate for themselves. Now, let it be borne in mind that every abolitionist and freesoiler, who

---

From Robert W. Johannsen, ed., *The Letters of Stephen A. Douglas* (Urbana: University of Illinois Press, 1961), 284–290.

opposes the Nebraska bill, allows his willingness to support it, provided that slavery shall be forever prohibited therein. The objection, therefore, does not consist in denial of the necessity for a territorial government, nor of the capacity of the people to govern themselves, so far as white men are concerned. They are willing to allow the people to legislate for themselves in relation to husband and wife, parent and child, master and servant, and guardian and ward, so far as white persons are to be affected; but seem to think that it requires a higher degree of civilization and refinement to legislate for the negro race than can reasonably be expected the people of a Territory to possess. Is this position well founded? Does it require any greater capacity or keener sense of moral rectitude to legislate for the black man than for the white man? Not being able to appreciate the force of this theory on the part of the abolitionists. I propose, by the express terms of the Nebraska bill, to leave the people of the Territories "perfectly free to form and regulate their domestic institutions in their own way, subject only to the Constitution of the United States."

. . .

The bill provides in words as specific and unequivocal as our language affords that the *true intent and meaning* of the act is NOT to legislate slavery into any Territory or State. The bill, therefore, does not introduce slavery; does not revive it; does not establish it; does not contain any clause designed to produce that result, or which by any possible construction can have that legal effect.

"Non-intervention by Congress with slavery in the States and Territories" is expressly declared to be the principle upon which the bill is constructed. The great fundamental principle of self-government, which authorizes the people to regulate their own domestic concerns, as recognized in the Compromise measure of 1850, and affirmed by the Democratic national convention, and reaffirmed by the Whig convention at Baltimore, is declared in this bill to be the rule of action in the formation of territorial governments. The two great political parties of the country are solemnly pledged to a strict adherence to this principle as a final settlement of the slavery question. How can that settlement be final, unless the principle be preserved and carried out in all new territorial organizations?

But the professed friend of the measure in the article referred to follows the lead of his abolition confederates in this city, and declares that this bill opens that whole country to slavery! Why do they not state the matter truly, and say that it opens the country to *freedom* by leaving the people *perfectly free* to do as they please? Is it true, as these professed advocates of freedom would wish to make the world believe, that the people of northern latitudes are so adverse to free institutions, and so much in love with slavery, that it is necessary to have Congress appointed their guardian in order to preserve that freedom of which they boast so much? Were not the people of New Hampshire left free to decide this question for themselves? Did not all the New England States become free States under the operation of the principle upon which the Nebraska bill is predicated? If this be so— and every child knows that it is true—by what authority are we told that a country lying between the same parallels of latitude which embrace all of the New England States, is to be doomed to slavery if we intrust them with the same rights, privileges, and immunities which the Constitution guarantees to the people of New England? Are the sons of New England any less capable of judging for themselves when they emigrate to Minnesota, Nebraska, or Kansas, than they were before they ever passed beyond that circle which circumscribed their vision with their native valleys? Is it wise to violate the great principle of self-government, which lies at the foundation of all free institutions, by constituting ourselves the officious guardians of a people we do not know, and of a country we never saw? May we not safely leave them to form and regulate their domestic institutions in the same manner, and by virtue of the same principle which enabled New York, New Jersey, and Pennsylvania to exclude slavery from their limits and establish free institutions for themselves?

But, sir, I fear I have already made this letter too long. If so, my apology therefore is to be found in the great importance of the subject, and my earnest desire that no honest mind be misled with regard to the provisions of the bill or the principles involved in it. Every intelligent man knows that it is a matter of no practical importance, so far as the question of slavery is concerned. The cry of the extension of slavery has been raised for mere party purposes by the abolition confederates and disappointed office-seekers. All candid men who understand the subject admit that the laws climate, and production, and of physical geography, (to use the language of one of New England's greatest statesmen), have excluded slavery from that country. This was admitted by Mr. Everett in his speech against the bill, and because slavery could not go there, he appealed to southern Senators not to insist upon applying the provisions of the Utah bill to Nebraska, when they would derive no advantages from it. The same admission and appeal were made by Mr. Smith, of Connecticut, in his speech against the bill. To-day, Mr. Badger, of North Carolina, replied to these appeals by the distinct declaration that he and his southern friends did not expect that slavery would go there; that the climate and productions were not adapted to slave labor; but they insisted upon it as a matter of principle, and of principle alone. In short, all candid and intelligent men make the same admission, and present the naked question as a matter of principle, whether the people shall be allowed to regulate their domestic concerns in their own way or not. In conclusion, I may be permitted to add, that the Democratic party, as well as the country, have a deep interest in this matter. Is our party to be again divided and rent asunder upon this vexed question of slavery?

Everything in the past history of the democracy of New Hampshire gives confidence and assurance to their patriotic brethren throughout the Union in a crisis like the present. I believe I know enough of the intelligence. consistency, and firmness of her people, to warrant the belief that while her favorite and honored son stands, as he has stood and now stands, firmly at the helm of the ship of state, calmly facing the threatening danger, regardless of all personal consequences, her noble people at home will sustain themselves and him against the attacks of open foes and the insidious assaults of pretended friends.

You will do me the justice to publish this in your next number. I have the honor to be, very respectfully, your obedient servant,
S. A. DOUGLAS

DRAWING CONCLUSION:

1. What can we learn from this document about the ways that Northern Democrats like Douglas sought to find a middle ground between the free soil and southern rights positions?

1.4 ABRAHAM LINCOLN, INTRODUCTION TO THE "HOUSE DIVIDED" SPEECH (1858)

In 1858, Abraham Lincoln received the Republican nomination to challenge the incumbent Democrat Stephen Douglass for a seat in the United States Senate. Lincoln and the Republicans made the issue of slavery's expansion the centerpiece of the campaign and argued that Douglas' popular sovereignty stance represented a tacit endorsement of the spread of slavery. This document presents the opening of Lincoln's acceptance speech to the Illinois state Republican convention that had just nominated him for Senate. In this opening segment, Lincoln lays out the central theme of his campaign and takes direct aim at Douglas and the principle of popular sovereignty.

GUIDING QUESTIONS:

1. What does Lincoln say is the central issue confronting the United States? What decision does he say Americans must make?
2. What implicit criticism is he making of Douglas and the principle of popular sovereignty in this speech?

INTRODUCTION TO THE "HOUSE DIVIDED" SPEECH

Abraham Lincoln
June 16, 1858

Mr. President and Gentlemen of the Convention:

If we could first know where we are and whither we are tending, we could better judge what to do and how to do it. We are now far into the fifth year since a policy was initiated with the avowed object and confident promise of putting an end to slavery agitation. Under the operation of that policy, that agitation has not only not ceased but has constantly augmented. In my opinion, it will not cease until a crisis shall have been reached and passed. "A house divided against itself cannot stand." I believe this government cannot endure, permanently, half slave and half free.

I do not expect the Union to be dissolved; I do not expect the house to fall; but I do expect it will cease to be divided. It will become all one thing, or all the other. Either the opponents of slavery will arrest the further spread of it and place it where the public mind shall rest in the belief that it is in the course of ultimate extinction, or its advocates will push it forward till it shall become alike lawful in all the states, old as well as new, North as well as South.

DRAWING CONCLUSION:

1. What can we learn from this document about the ways that Republicans responded to the efforts of Northern Democrats like Douglas to find a middle ground between the free soil and southern rights positions?

CASE STUDY—THE CANING
OF CHARLES SUMNER

Charles Sumner was a Republican Senator from Massachusetts who had deep roots in the abolitionist movement and was among the most outspoken anti-slavery voices in Congress. In May of 1856, Sumner delivered a fiery anti-slavery speech entitled "The Crime Against Kansas" on the Senate floor. In the speech, Sumner denounced the efforts to bring Kansas into the Union as a slave state. Under the terms of the Kansas-Nebraska Act, white settlers would be the ones to determine the status of slavery in Kansas. In late 1855 and early 1856, violence erupted between pro- and anti-slavery settlers in Kansas and escalated into a low-level civil war. Republicans in the North denounced the tactics of pro-slavery settlers and turned "Bleeding Kansas" into a potent political issue. Sumner's speech was part of this ongoing effort by Republicans to focus public attention on the violence in Kansas.

Near the start of the speech Sumner took the opportunity to denounce Senators Andrew Butler of South Carolina and Stephen Douglas of Illinois in highly personal terms. Two days after the speech, Butler's cousin Representative Preston Brooks of South Carolina approached Sumner in the Senate chambers as he was working at his desk. After accusing Sumner of libel against South Carolina and against Butler, Brooks beat Sumner repeatedly with a walking cane until Sumner was left bloodied and unconscious. Sumner's injuries were so severe that it would be two years before he could return to his seat in the Senate.

The caning of Sumner provoked a storm of outrage across the North. Many in the South, by contrast, defended Brooks. The Republican Party made effective use of the twin issues of "Bleeding Kansas" and "Bleeding Sumner" in the fall 1856 presidential and congressional campaigns to establish themselves as the dominant party in the North. The caning of Sumner thus helped place the United States on the path that led to the election of Abraham Lincoln to the presidency in 1860, to secession, and to war. The caning, however, is also an excellent case study through which to explore the growing sectional polarization of American politics in the 1850s. The documents presented include an excerpt from Sumner's speech as well as examples of the reactions of people both in the North and the South to the incident. As you examine these documents, ask yourself why those in the North and the South reacted to the caning as they did, how politicians used the incident to their advantage, and what the episode reveals about the factors driving the sectional polarization of American politics.

2.1 FROM CHARLES SUMNER, "THE CRIME AGAINST KANSAS" (1856)

This document presents the section of Sumner's speech that provoked Preston Brooks' assault. As you read this excerpt, do not be concerned with understanding every literary and historical allusion that Sumner employs. Instead, ask yourself why Brooks took such great offense on behalf of his uncle. In the speech, Sumner is mocking both Andrew Butler and Stephen Douglas. What exactly is he saying about Butler? Pay particular attention, for instance, to Sumner's sexual allusions, such as his use of the term "harlot," which is an archaic synonym for "prostitute." It will also be helpful to have some knowledge of Sumner's central metaphor, which is drawn from the story of Don Quixote made famous in the novel of that name by the renowned Spanish author Miguel de Cervantes. Don Quixote is the story of a Spanish nobleman who loses his sanity and imagines himself a chivalric knight. In the company of Sancho Panza, a simple farmer that Don Quixote deems his squire, he embarks on a quest to undo the wrongs of the world. Don Quixote dedicates his quest to Aldonza Lorenzo, a local peasant that he imagines to be a beautiful noblewoman named Dulcinea del Toboso. In comparing Butler to Don Quixote, Sumner intends to mock the South Carolina's senator's pretensions to nobility.

GUIDING QUESTION:

1. What is Charles Sumner saying about Andrew Butler in this speech? Keep in mind that he is engaging in mockery.

THE CRIME AGAINST KANSAS

My task will be divided under three different heads; *first*, THE CRIME AGAINST KANSAS, in its origin and extent; *secondly*, THE APOLOGIES FOR THE CRIME; and *thirdly*, the TRUE REMEDY.

But, before entering upon the argument, I must say something of a general character, particularly in response to what has fallen from Senators who have raised themselves to eminence on this floor in championship of human wrongs; I mean the Senator from South Carolina, [Mr. BUTLER,] and the Senator from Illinois, [Mr. DOUGLAS,] who, though unlike as Don Quixote and Sancho Panza, yet, like this couple, sally forth together in the same adventure. I regret much to miss the elder Senator from his seat; but the cause, against which he has run a tilt, with such activity of animosity, demands that the opportunity of exposing him should not be lost; and it is for the cause that I speak. The Senator from South Carolina has read many books of chivalry, and believes himself a chivalrous knight, with sentiments of honor and courage. Of course he has chosen a mistress to whom he has made his vows, and who, though ugly to others, is always lovely to him; though polluted in the sight of the world, is chaste in his sight—I mean the harlot, Slavery. For her, his tongue is always profuse in words. Let her be impeached in character, or any proposition made to shut her out from the extension of her wantonness, and no extravagance of manner or hardihood of assertion is then too great for this Senator. The frenzy of Don Quixote, in behalf of his wench Dulcinea del Toboso, is all surpassed. The asserted rights of Slavery, which shock equality of all

From Charles Sumner, *The Kansas Question* (Cincinnati: George S. Blanchard, 1856), 5–7.

kinds, are cloaked by a fantastic claim of equality. If the slave States cannot enjoy what, in mockery of the great fathers of the Republic, he misnames equality under the Constitution—in other words, the full power in the National Territories to compel fellowmen to unpaid toil, to separate husband and wife, and to sell little children at the auction block—then, sir, the chivalric Senator will conduct the State of South Carolina out of the Union! Heroic knight! Exalted Senator! A second Moses come for a second exodus!

But not content with this poor menace, which we have been twice told was "measured," the Senator, in the unrestrained chivalry of his nature, has undertaken to apply opprobrious words to those who differ from him on this floor. He calls them "sectional and fanatical:" and opposition to the usurpation in Kansas, he denounces as "an uncalculating fanaticism." To be sure, these charges lack all grace of originality, and all sentiment of truth; but the adventurous Senator does not hesitate. He is the uncompromising, unblushing representative on this floor of a flagrant *sectionalism*, which now domineers over the Republic, and yet with a ludicrous ignorance of his own position—unable to see himself as others see him—or with an effrontery which even his white head ought not to protect from rebuke, he applies to those here who resist his *sectionalism* the very epithet which designates himself. The men who strive to bring back the Government to its original policy, when Freedom and not Slavery was national, while Slavery and not Freedom was sectional, he arraigns as *sectional*. This will not do. It involves too great a perversion of terms. I tell that Senator, that it is to himself, and to the "organization" of which he is the "committed advocate," that this epithet belongs. I now fasten it upon them. For myself, I care little for names; but since the question has been raised here, I affirm that the Republican party of the Union is in no just sense *sectional*, but, more than any other party, *national*, and that it now goes forth to dislodge from the high places of the Government the tyrannical sectionalism of which the Senator from South Carolina is one of the maddest zealots.

To the charge of fanaticism I also reply. Sir, fanaticism is found in an enthusiasm or exaggeration of opinions, particularly on religious subjects; but

there may be a fanaticism for evil as well as for good. Now, I will not deny, that there are persons among us loving Liberty too well for their personal good, in a selfish generation. Such there may be, and, for the sake of their example, would that there were more! In calling them "fanatics," you cast contumely upon the noble army of martyrs, from the earliest day down to this hour; Upon the great tribunes of human rights, by whom life, liberty, and happiness, on earth, have been secured; upon the long line of devoted patriots, who, throughout history, have truly loved their country; and, upon all, who, in noble aspirations for the general good and in forgetfulness of self, have stood out before their age, and gathered into their generous bosoms the shafts of tyranny and wrong, in order to make a pathway for Truth. You discredit Luther, when alone he nailed his articles to the door of the church at Wittenberg, and then, to the imperial demand that he should retract, firmly replied, "Here I stand; I cannot do otherwise, so help me God!" You discredit Hampden, when alone he refused to pay the few shillings of ship-money, and shook the throne of Charles I; you discredit Milton, when, amidst the corruptions of a heartless Court, he lived on, the lofty friend of Liberty, above question or suspicion; you discredit Russell and Sidney, when, for the sake of their country, they calmly turned from family and friends, to tread the narrow steps of the scaffold; you discredit those early founders of American institutions, who preferred the hardships of a wilderness, surrounded by a savage foe, to injustice on beds of ease; you discredit our later fathers, who, few in numbers and weak in resources, yet strong in their cause, did not hesitate to brave the mighty power of England, already encircling the globe with her morning drumbeats. Yes, sir, of such are the fanatics of history, according to the Senator. But I tell that Senator, that there are characters badly eminent, of whose fanaticism there can be no question. Such were the ancient Egyptians, who worshipped divinities in brutish forms; the Druids, who darkened the forests of oak, in which they lived, by sacrifices of blood; the Mexicans, who surrendered countless victims to the propitiation of their obscene idols; the Spaniards, who, under Alva, sought to force the Inquisition upon Holland, by a tyranny kindred to that now employed to force Slavery upon Kansas; and such were the Algerines, when in solemn conclave, after listening to a speech not unlike that of the Senator from South Carolina, they resolved to continue the slavery of white Christians, and to extend it to the countrymen of Washington! Aye, sir, extend it! And in this same dreary catalogue faithful history must record all who now, in an enlightened age and in a land of boasted Freedom, stand up, in perversion of the Constitution and in denial of immortal truth, to fasten a new shackle upon their fellow-man. If the Senator wishes to see fanatics, let him look round among his own associates; let him look at himself.

But I have not done with the Senator. There is another matter regarded by him of such consequence, that he interpolated it into the speech of the Senator from New Hampshire, [Mr. HALE,] and also announced that he had prepared himself with it, to take in his pocket all the way to Boston, when he expected to address the people of that community. On this account, and for the sake of truth, I stop for one moment, and tread it to the earth. The North, according to the Senator, was engaged in the slave trade, and helped to introduce slaves into the Southern States; and this undeniable fact he proposed to establish by statistics, in stating which his errors surpassed his sentences in number. But I let these pass for the present, that I may deal with his argument. Pray, sir, is the acknowledged turpitude of a departed generation to become an example for us? And yet the suggestion of the Senator, if entitled to any consideration in this discussion, must have this extent. I join my friend from New Hampshire in thanking the Senator from South Carolina for adducing this instance; for it gives me an opportunity to say, that the Northern merchants, with homes in Boston, Bristol, Newport, New York, and Philadelphia, who catered for Slavery during the years of the slave trade, are the lineal progenitors of the Northern men, with homes in these places, who lend themselves to Slavery in our day; and especially that all, whether North or South, who take part, directly or indirectly, in the conspiracy against Kansas, do but continue the work of the slave-traders, which you condemn. It is true, too true, alas! that our fathers were engaged in this traffic; but that is no apology for it. And in repelling the authority of

this example, I repel also the trite argument founded on the earlier example of England. It is true that our mother country, at the peace of Utrecht, extorted from Spain the Assiento Contract, securing the monopoly of the slave trade with the Spanish Colonies, as the whole price of all the blood of great victories; that she higgled at Aix-la-Chapelle for another lease of this exclusive traffic; and again, at the treaty of Madrid, clung to the wretched piracy. It is true that in this spirit the power of the mother country was prostituted to the same base ends in her American Colonies, against indignant protests from our fathers. All these things now rise up in judgment against her. Let us not follow the Senator from South Carolina to do the very evil to day, which in another generation we condemn.

As the Senator from South Carolina is the Don Quixote, the Senator from Illinois [Mr. DOUGLAS] is the squire of Slavery, its very Sancho Panza, ready to do all its humiliating offices. This Senator, in his labored address, vindicating his labored report—piling one mass of elaborate error upon another mass—constrained himself, as you will remember, to unfamiliar decencies of speech. Of that address I have nothing to say at this moment, though before I sit down I shall show something of its fallacies. But I go back now to an earlier occasion, when, true to his native impulses, he threw into this discussion, "for a charm of powerful trouble," personalities most discreditable to this body. I will not stop to repel the imputations, which he cast upon myself; but I mention them to remind you of the "sweltered venom sleeping got," which, with other poisoned ingredients, he cast into the cauldron of this debate. Of other things I speak. Standing on this floor, the Senator issued his rescript, requiring submission to the Usurped Power of Kansas; and this was accompanied by a manner all his own—such as befits the tyrannical threat. Very well. Let the Senator try. I tell him now that he cannot enforce any such submission. The Senator, with the Slave Power at his back, is strong; but he is not strong enough for this purpose. He is bold. He shrinks from nothing. Like Danton, he may cry, *"l'audace! l'audace! toujours l'audace!"* but even his audacity cannot compass this work. The Senator copies the British officer, who, with boastful swagger, said that with the hilt of his sword he would cram the "stamps" down the throats of the American people, and he will meet a similar failure. He may convulse this country with civil feud. Like the ancient madman, he may set fire to this Temple of Constitutional Liberty, grander than Ephesian dome; but he cannot enforce obedience to that tyrannical Usurpation.

The Senator dreams that he can subdue the North. He disclaims the open threat, but his conduct still implies it. How little that Senator knows himself, or the strength of the cause which he persecutes! He is but a mortal man; against him is an immortal principle. With finite power he wrestles with the infinite, and he must fall. Against him are stronger battalions than any marshaled by mortal arm—the inborn, ineradicable, invincible sentiments of the human heart; against him is nature in all her subtle forces; against him is God. Let him try to subdue these.

DRAWING CONCLUSION:

1. Why might Preston Brooks have taken such great offense at Charles Sumner's mockery of his uncle, Andrew Butler? What does this suggest about the cultural values to which Brooks subscribed?

2.2 SOUTHERN RESPONSES TO THE CANING OF SUMNER

These editorials and news reports from southern newspapers document southern reactions to the caning of Charles Sumner. The documents demonstrate widespread sympathy for Brooks, even among those who did not endorse his specific actions, as well as a substantial body of support for the attack itself. The documents also demonstrate enormous hostility toward Charles Sumner and, by extension, the anti-slavery voices in the North that Sumner spoke for. The articles are drawn from a variety of parts of the South and from newspapers with diverse partisan identifications. (In the nineteenth-century, American newspapers openly identified with specific political parties.)

GUIDING QUESTIONS

1. How is Charles Sumner portrayed in these articles?
2. What justifications are provided for Brooks's assault on Sumner in these documents?

NEW ORLEANS *DAILY CRESCENT*, MAY 29, 1856

WASHINGTON CORRESPONDENCE

[From Our Special Correspondent]
Washington, May 22d, 1856

The debate in the Senate on Tuesday, and the gross personalities which it gave rise to, have been the subject of general comment.—It originated in an elaborate speech from Sumner, of Massachusetts, on the Kansas question. Were it not for ocular proof to the contrary, it would be difficult to believe that Sumner belonged to the human family. A more dirty, disgusting, and offensive specimen of degraded humanity than this man, never polluted the air of Heaven. His speech was little else than a tissue of accusations and reproaches of all those members of the Senate who are not leagued with him in his diabolical treason. He did not hesitate to denounce them as swindlers; liars and ruffians. He availed himself of the absence of Judge Butler, of South Carolina—one of the purest and best men of the country—to charge him with falsehood and prevarication. In a word, he blackguarded three-fourths of his senatorial associates. When he closed, he was severely rebuked by General Cass, Judge Douglas, and Mr. Mason. But it had no more effect upon him than a lecture on decency would have upon a skunk. He sat smiling and smirking as if he rather enjoyed it than otherwise.

It is difficult to say how such men should be treated. No amount of insult can goad them to personal resistance. Indeed, they prefer that they should seem to be martyrs to their faith. If Sumner or Seward could get kicked or spit upon, it would be worth a re-election to the Senate—and hence, they court insults rather than avoid them. In private, they are tabooed and unrecognized. No man with any pretensions to the character of a gentleman, would be caught in the street with such men as Sumner or Hale. But, in the Senate, they appear to enjoy abuse—and omit no opportunity of provoking it by slanders upon others. It is a shame and a burning disgrace to the Republic, that such a man as Sumner should occupy a seat in the halls of our legislature-and that *gentlemen* should be compelled to come even into *political* contact with him.

RICHMOND *ENQUIRER*, JUNE 2, 1856

"In the main, the press of the South applaud the conduct of Mr. Brooks, without condition or limitation. Our approbation at least is entire and unreserved. We consider the net good in conception, better in execution, and best of all in consequences. These vulgar abolitionists in the Senate are *getting above themselves*. They have been humored until they forget their position. They have grown *saucy*, and *dare to be impudent to gentlemen*. Now they are a low, mean, scurvy set, with some little book learning, but as utterly devoid of spirit and honor as a pack of curs. Intrenched behind 'privilege,' they fancy they can slander the South and its representatives with impunity."

"The truth is, they have been suffered to run too long without *collars*. They must be *lashed into submission*. Sumner, in particular, ought to have nine-and-thirty early every morning. He is a strapping young fellow, and could stand the *cowhide* beautifully. Brooks frightened him, and, at the first blow of the *cane*, he hollowed like a bull-calf.

"There is the blackguard *Wilson*, all ignorant Natick cobbler, swaggering in excess of muscle, and, absolutely dying for a beating. Will not somebody take him in hand? Hale is another huge, red-faced, sweating scoundrel, whom some gentleman should *kick* and *cuff* until he abates something of his impudent talk.

"We trust other gentlemen will follow the example of Mr. Brooks, that so a curb may be imposed upon the truculence and audacity of abolition speakers. If need be, let us have a *caning* or *cowhiding* every day. If the worst come to the worst, so much the sooner, so much the better."

ACCOUNT OF PUBLIC MEETING IN ABBEVILLE, SOUTH CAROLINA

PUBLIC MEETING.

Pursuant to notice previously given, a very large assemblage of the most intelligent, respectable and influential citizens of this District, convened in the Court House this morning at 11 o'clock, to give an expression of opinion as to the late occurrence between the HON. PRESTON S. BROOKS, of this Congressional District, and CHARLES SUMNER, Senator from Massachusetts, in the Senate Chamber of the United States.

After the meeting was brought to order, the Hon. J. FOSTER MARSHALL was called to the Chair, and R.A. FAIR requested to act as Secretary.

The object of the meeting being explained by the Chair in a few well timed and eloquent remarks, the meeting was declared ready to proceed to business.

Whereupon, Edward Noble, Esq., arose and read the following Preamble and Resolutions, the adoption of which he recommended in a speech of some length and great merit, to wit:

WHEREAS, late intelligence from Washington informs us that a Senator from Massachusetts, Charles Sumner, on the 19th and 20th of May, in the Senate, made a deliberate and dastardly attack upon the character of our distinguished and venerable Senator, Mr. Butler, and at the same time, with tongue dripping with venom, he defamed and insulted the State of South Carolina, falsifying her history, denouncing her constitution, and with every epithet of insult, abuse and defamation, assaulting her honor.

In consequence of this outrage upon South Carolina, and assault upon Mr. Butler, who was absent from the Senate, the Hon. P. S. Brooks, our immediate Representative, in vindicating the former, the tender and fostering mother of us all, and the latter, a near and venerable kinsman of his, administered on the 22d of May, upon the very spot where the outrage had been committed, a deserved, merited and spirited caning upon the person of the said Senator from Massachusetts, Mr. Sumner. Therefore,

Be it unanimously resolved by this meeting, That as a token of our approval of his conduct, we tender to our distinguished Representative our cordial support, and signify to him our approval of his conduct in the premises.

Resolved, As a substantial testimonial of our approbation, we present our distinguished Representative with a Gold Goblet, with an appropriate inscription thereupon, and that a committee of three be appointed to procure the Goblet, and in the name of this District to present it to him, together with a copy of these Resolutions.

The adoption of the Resolutions was also urged by Dr. Paul Conner, Maj. J.K. Vance, Dr. S.V. Cain, Gen. S. McGowan, Thos. Thomson, Esq., Maj. H.A. Jones, C.T. Haskel, Esq., Cols. A.M. Smith, T. C. Perrin, John A. Calhoun, Dr. George W. Presley and others, in short

---

From the Abbeville (South Carolina) *Banner*, June 5, 1856

but effective and patriotic speeches, fully endorsing the spirited and manly conduct of our chivalrous Representative in the premises.

The Preamble and Resolutions being submitted to the meeting, were unanimously adopted.

Upon a call from the Chair, the money for the purchase of the testimonial was immediately furnished by the meeting.

Edward Noble, Esq., Gen. S. McGowan and Maj. H.A. Jones were appointed by the Chair the committee of three under the *second resolution*.

On motion of Dr. Cain, it was

Resolved, That the proceedings of this meeting be published in our District papers. The meeting was then adjourned.

J. FOSTER MARSHALL, *Chm.*
F.A. FAIR, *Sec.*
Abbeville C.H., June 2, 1856.

ACCOUNT OF MEETING OF THE MEDICAL CLASS AT THE UNIVERSITY OF NASHVILLE

NASHVILLE *UNION AND AMERICAN*, JUNE 5, 1856

TO THE EDITORS.

Medical Hall, Nashville, Tenn., June 3, 1856.

At a meeting of the medical class of the University of Nashville, E. M. Dupree, of South Carolina, was called to the chair and J. Maclin Driver requested to act as secretary. The following gentlemen were appointed Vice Presidents, J. R. G. Fawcette, of North Carolina, George T. Turner, of Georgia, D. H. Armstrong, of Mississippi, Nathan Miller, of Alabama, W. G. A. Daniel, of Texas, J. W. Williamson, of Kentucky, and C. H. Mullins, of Tennessee.

On motion, a committee of five, consisting of Messrs. L. J. Applewhite and M. D. Blanchard, of Georgia, Newton C. Miller, M. D. Kelly, and S. S. Porter, of Tennessee, were appointed to draft resolutions expressive of the sense of the meeting. After retiring a few minutes, the committee returned and reported through their chairman, L. J. Applewhite, the following preamble and resolutions, which were unanimously adopted:

Whereas, we have heard of the recent attack of the P. S. Brooks, of South Carolina, upon Senator Sumner, of Massachusetts, on the floor of the Senate of the United States; and whereas we deem it fit to give an expression of our opinion relative thereto: Therefore

Resolved, That we have read with indignation the speech of Senator Sumner, recently delivered in the Senate of the United States, in which language is employed and sentiments indulged in towards Honorable Senators, crossly personal and abusive, and unbecoming a man occupying the high and dignified position of a senator in Congress.

Resolved. That for Chas. Sumner, Senator in Congress from Massachusetts, as a man, we have the most unmitigated contempt, and that we regard his political course as unpatriotic in the extreme, and as deserving the condemnation of all honorable men.

Resolved, That the doctrine of freedom of debate is a wholesome one, but was never intended as a screen for unprincipled men, under protection of which, to heap insult and abuse upon their compeers with impunity.

Resolved, That the circumstances provoking the attack were of the most aggravated character, and we fully appreciate the motives governing the Hon. P. S. Brooks in making the attack, and that whilst we do not approve of the course of this gentleman in making the assault in the Senate Chamber, yet we think the circumstances which provoked it go far in mitigation of the act.

Resolved, That we do not regard the assault of Hon. P. S. Brooks as a sufficient cause for his expulsion from the House, and that we think this act would be a piece of great injustice to the State which sent him there, and would be an event unprecedented in the annals of American deliberative bodies.

Resolved, That the city papers be requested to publish the proceedings of this meeting.

E. M. Dupree, President
J. Maclin Driver, Secretary.

DRAWING CONCLUSIONS:

1. What do these documents reveal about southern responses to the growing anti-slavery sentiment in the North?
2. What do these documents reveal about the cultural values of the white South?

2.3   NORTHERN RESPONSES TO THE CANING OF SUMNER

These editorials and news reports from northern newspapers document northern reactions to the caning of Charles Sumner. The documents demonstrate widespread outrage in the North, even among those who disagreed bitterly with Sumner politically. Pay particular attention to the ways Republicans used this outrage to mobilize broader anti-slavery and anti-slave owner sentiment. The articles are drawn from a variety of parts of the North and from newspapers with diverse partisan identifications. (In the nineteenth-century, American newspapers openly identified with specific political parties.) The partisan affiliations of the newspapers are provided where available.

GUIDING QUESTIONS:

1. How is the caning of Charles Sumner portrayed in these articles?
2. How is the culture of the white South and of slave owners portrayed in these articles, particularly by Republicans?

NEW YORK TRIBUNE, MAY 24, 1856
(REPUBLICAN)

The assault on Senator Sumner reverberates through the land, causing throughout the Free States the intensest excitement and indignation. Other men have been as causelessly assailed, and are wantonly, if not as savagely, beaten; but the knocking down and beating to bloody blindness and unconsciousness of an American Senator while writing at his desk in the Senate Chamber is a novel illustration of the ferocious Southern spirit. It carries home to myriads of understandings a more vivid, if not a wholly original perception, of the degradation in which the Free States have consented for years to exist. The degradation was as real years ago, but never before so palpable as now. When a citizen of a Northern State so thoroughly subservient to the Slave Power as Edward Everett could be opposed in the Senate and well nigh rejected as Minister to England, because he had once, under the pressure of a strong local feeling, avowed, as a candidate for Congress, some abstract opposition to Slavery, it was high time for the North to unite in declaring that this sort of inquisition must be stopped—that, so long as devotion to Slavery was not made a barrier to Executive

station, devotion to Freedom should not be. But the North has always lacked manly self-assertion, especially in the Senate, where a majority of her nominal representatives voted, only a few weeks since, to kick out the petition of Free Kansas for admission, on some paltry pretext of informality, and surrender her citizens to the unchecked brutalities and inflamed indignation of the Border Ruffians.

The beating of private citizens or the butchery of Irish waiters by the Southern Oligarchy, have made no impression on the public mind at all comparable in breadth or vividness with that which has been and will be produced by the assault of which Mr. Sumner has been the victim. Widely known in both hemispheres as among the first of American scholars and orators, his career as a Senator has conferred renown even on the glorious commonwealth of which he is the foremost representative. Elected as the champion of no interest, no clique, no party, but simply of the great idea of Impartial Freedom, he has been eminently faithful to his high calling. Nobody could infer from his votes or speeches that he was ever, in the party sense, a Whig or a Democrat; but no one can doubt that he is an earnest and fearless condemner of Slavery. But four years in public life, he has already done much to redeem the term Abolitionist from the unmerited odium which an era of baseness, self-seeking and infidelity to Revolutionary tradition and Republican principle has contrived to cast upon it. He has elevated the range and widened the scope of Senatorial debate, summoning Poetry and Literature to the elucidation of the gravest and dryest political propositions while by careful preparation and a finished oratory he has attracted thousands to hear and to consider elemental truths with the enunciation of which the corrupt and servile atmosphere of the Federal metropolis has been agitated far too seldom. There is no man now living who within the last five years has rendered the American People greater service or won for himself a nobler fame than Charles Sumner.

It is high time that this People should take a stand not only against the immediate perpetrators of ruffian assaults but against their confederates and apologists in public life and in the Press. As long as words sincerely spoken can be pleaded as an apology for blows, we shall be recorded by impartial observers as barbarians—and justly so regarded. So long as our truly civilized and refined communities succumb to the rule of the barbarian elements in our political system, we must be judged by the character and conduct of our accepted masters. The youth trained to knock down his human chattels for "insolence"—that is for any sort of resistance to his good pleasure—will thereafter knock down and beat other human beings who thwart his wishes—no matter whether they be Irish waiters or New England Senators. Once admit the idea of the predominance of brute force—of the right of individual appeal from words to blows—and human society becomes a state of war, diversified by interludes of fitful and hollow truce. And they who, as legislators, editors, public speakers, or in whatever capacity, suggest apologies for ruffian assaults, or intimate that words *can* excuse them, make themselves partners in the crime and the infamy.

CORRESPONDENCE
Indignation Meeting in Hinesburgh
Hinesburgh, May 29th, 1856

The citizens of Hinesburgh met, pursuant to a call to that effect, in Convention at the Town Hall, in said Town, for the purpose of taking into consideration the late outrages upon the rights of Freemen, both in Kansas and in our National Legislature.

The Convention was duly organized by the appointment of H. Toby, as Chairman, and A. E. Leavenworth, as Secretary.

After appropriate remarks, expressive of the object of the call, and that it is the imperative duty of the friends of freedom in these United States, to take immediate and energetic action in the premises: Hon. Francis Willson, Hon. Jos. Marsh and Dr. Jno. F. Miles were appointed a committee to prepare and report resolutions, expressive of the sense of this meeting.

The committee, after consultation, reported, substantially, the following resolutions, which after an animated discussion, were adopted by acclamation.

Resolved, by the citizens of Hinesburgh in convention assembled, that the period has arrived, when it becomes the imperative duty of every citizen to solemnly contemplate the momentous events that are transpiring in our country. That we yield to none in our ardent attachment to the principles laid down In the constitution of these United States—that freedom of thought, freedom of speech, and freedom of action so far as does not violate the organic laws of the land, are rights secured to us as inalienable and inviolate.

Resolved, That the attack of Preston S. Brooks, Member of Congress from S. C. upon the person of Hon. Charles Sumner in the Senate Chamber of the United States, was unjustifiable, wanton and cowardly and exhibits the same spirit that is manifested by the Border Ruffians of Kansas.

Resolved, That the enormous outrages of the slave power, committed upon unoffending freemen in Kansas, and sanctioned by the present administration, call upon all lovers of freedom and good order,

Burlington (Vermont) *Free Press*, June 6, 1856 (Republican)

to rebuke such power and administration, by the legislative acts of each state.

Resolved, That in our opinion, his excellency the Governor of Vermont, will be fully justified in convening the Hon. legislature of this State a soon as may be, to take such action in regard to the aforesaid outrages as their wisdom shall suggest.

Resolved, That the time has arrived, when the citizens of this state should meet in solemn council. We would therefore recommend that a mass meeting be called to be held in Burlington at as early a day as practicable, to mutually contemplate our national affairs, and recommend such measures as may be demanded.

On motion of Rev. C. L. Ferrin, the meeting ordered that a copy of these proceedings be immediately forwarded to the "Burlington Free Press" for publication.

On motion, the meeting adjourned until Monday evening, June 2d, at 6 o'clock.

H. Toby, Chairman
(Attest,) A. E. Leavenworth, Secretary

PORTAGE SENTINEL (RAVENNA, OHIO), MAY 29, 1856 (DEMOCRATIC)

Outrage on Mr. Sumner.

A few day ago, CHARLES SUMNER, U.S. Senator from Massachusetts, made a speech in the Senate, upon the Kansas question, in the course of which, he Indulged in bitter personalities towards several Senators, and particularly against Senator Butler of South Carolina. He charged the latter gentleman of falsehood, and used other language unbecoming and outrageous.

SENATOR BUTLER was absent. He is an old man—a man of amiable and courteous manners, and the attack of MR. SUMNER upon him was unjustifiable.

MR. BROOKS, a member of the House from South Carolina, and a relative of MR. BUTLERS, hearing of the affair entered the Senate Chamber where Sumner was sitting and struck him over the head with a cane, knocking him nearly senseless, and cutting his head and face badly. The blows were repeated until SUMNER was deprived of the power of speech. So says the telegraphic report.

This whole affair from the beginning to the end, is one of the most disgraceful which has ever occurred in the Senate. That our readers may form a just judgment in regard to the whole matter we give the following extract from MR. SUMNER's speech in reference to SENATOR BUTLER:

"With regret I come again upon the Senator from South Carolina, (Mr. Butler.) who omnipresent in this debate, overflowed with rage at the simple suggestion that Kansas had applied for admission as a State; and, with incoherent phrases, discharged the loose expectoration of din speech, now upon her representative, and then upon her people—There was no extravagance of the ancient parliamentary debate which he did not repent; nor was there any possible deviation from truth which he did not make, with so much of passion, I am glad to add, as to save him from the suspicion of intentional aberration. Because the Senator touches nothing which he does not disfigure with error, sometime of principle, Sometimes of fact. He shows an *incapacity of accuracy,* whether in stating the constitution or in stating the law, whether in the details of statistics or the diversion of scholarship. He cannot open his mouth but out there flies a blunder."

Every honest man must admit that such language is unbecoming in the character of an American Senator, It sounds more like the billingsgate of the grog-shop, than the words of honorable debate between honorable men. Mr. SUMMER did wrong. He disgraced himself and the Senate. He disregarded the rules of courtesy which should ever characterize the conduct of a Senator. He allowed hatred and malice to bear rule as, it seems to us, no honorable man ever should.

Still this does not in any manner justify Mr. BROOKS. His attack upon Mr. Sumner was an outrage for which there is no possible justification. It was cowardly and mean. If the House of Representatives has any regard for its character; if its members have any respect for themselves, they will purge themselves from the stain, by expelling Brooks from that body. He is unworthy of a seat among the representatives of a free Government. While such men as he, are permitted to occupy stations of public trust and honor, neither the lives of the people or the institutions of the country are safe. He is guilty of an offense that is not only censurable, but criminal, and he should suffer the just penalty.

FROM THE *CLEVELAND HERALD* (WHIG)

SOUTHERN CHIVALRY.

We have had exhibited, during the present session of Congress, two precious specimens of Southern Chivalry. That boasted article amounts to this—a blow from behind. RUST from Alabama attacked HORACE GREELY, knowing that Mr. G. was physically a very weak man—nature having spent altogether more time in finishing of the brain than the arms and legs that he was near-sighted and that he was totally unarmed. Yet was this Alabama Ruffian coward enough to make his attack without a warning, and with a cane.

BROOKS, the South Carolina coward, squatted like an assassin beside the gate post to the Capitol rounds, to "get in" a blow upon Mr. SUMNER as he should pass; but thwarted in that plan, the Ruffian sneaked into the Senate Chamber, crouched behind the seats until the Chamber was nearly cleared, then coming up behind Senator SUMNER as he was wedged into his seat between a stationary desk and arm chair, dealt his unarmed sitting victim, a deadly blow, and felled him to the floor. This is Southern Chivalry! It is the chivalry of the assassin.

Men who habitually go armed are cowards, arrant cowards, and the custom of carrying deadly weapons, which prevails so extensively at the South, is the offspring of cowardice. The braggart will carry arms, hoping that fact will render his miserable carcass a defence his craven spirit refuses to yield; and be who knows he deserves a castigation and has not the moral courage to defend himself, will carry a pistol that the death of an antagonist may save him, the aggressor, from a flogging. What these men lack in moral courage and true bravery, they strive to supply with powder and ball.

There seems no other way than to meet these ruffians with their own weapons.—True, weapons would be of no avail in such a dastardly assault from behind as BROOKS made upon SUMNER, but it must be understood that Northern men are ready for these fellows. A ball through the brain of that South Carolinian BROOKS would have had greater moral effect than all resolutions of expulsion Congress could pass in a long session—*Cleveland Herald*

FROM THE *PITTSBURGH GAZETTE* (WHIG/REPUBLICAN)

THE ATTACK ON MR. SUMNER—The news of the cowardly attack on Mr. Sumner by a villainous South Carolinian, stirred up a deeper indignation among our citizens, yesterday, than we have ever before witnesses. It was an indignation that prevaded all classes and conditions of men. The assault was so deliberately planned, being made in the presence and under the encouragement of a crowd of bullies, when Mr. Sumner was alone, and unarmed and defenceless, and it was conducted so brutally fifty blows being inflicted upon an unresisting victim, until the weapon of attack was used up, and not one hand raised among the bystanders to stay the fury of the perfidious wretch, that every feeling of human nature revolts at the exhibition. Barbarians and ravages would not be guilty of such unmanliness; and even the vulgar blackguards who follow the business of bruisers and shoulder-hitters would have a far higher sense of fair play than was shown by these patterns of chivalry.

It is time now, to inaugurate a change. It can no longer be permitted that all the blows shall come from one side. If Southern men will resort to the fist to overawe and intimidate Northern men, blow must be given back for blow. Forbearance and kindly deportment are lost upon these Southern ruffians. It were as well to throw pearls before swine as turn one cheek to *them* when the other is smitten. Under the circumstances now prevailing, neither religion nor manhood requires submission to such outrages. Northern men must defend themselves; and if our present representatives will not fight, when attacked, let us find those who will. It is not enough, now, to have backbone; there must be strong right arms, and a determination to use them. The voters

---

Reprinted in the *Western Reserve Chronicle*, June 4, 1856.
Reprinted in the *Western Reserve Chronicle*, June 4, 1856.

of the free States, in vindication of their own manliness will, hereafter, in addition to inquiring of candidates: Will you vote so-and-so, have to enlarge the basis of interrogation, and demand an affirmative answer to the question, Will you fight? It has come to that, now, that Senators and Representatives cannot enjoy the right of free speech or free discussion, without being liable to brutal assaults; and they must, of necessity, arm themselves with swords-canes or revolvers. To think of enduring quietly such attacks as that upon Mr. Sumner is craven and pusillanimous. These cut-throat Southerns will never learn to respect Northern men until some one of their number has a rapier thrust through his ribs, or feels a bullet in his thorax. It is lamentable that such *should* be the case; but it is not in human nature be trampled on.

DRAWING CONCLUSIONS:

1. How did northern and southern reactions to the caning of Charles Sumner differ?
2. How did Republicans make use of the caning politically?
3. What do the contrasting reactions to the caning in the North and South reveal about the factors promoting the sectional polarization of American politics in the 1850s?

THE SECTIONALIZATION OF POLITICS—NATIONAL ELECTION RESULTS, 1836–1860

One way to track the sectional polarization of national politics is through an examination of presidential election results. The color coding on these maps indicate the victorious political party in each state for presidential elections between 1836 and 1860. Note that in the earlier elections, the two major parties (the Whigs and Democrats) were competitive throughout the country. By 1860, politics was split largely along north-south lines. The North was dominated by the Republican Party, a party with virtually no support in the South. Meanwhile, the South was dominated by the Democratic Party, and support for Democrats in the North had declined significantly. Furthermore, in 1860, the Democratic Party itself split into northern and southern wings, each of which ran its own candidate for president.

GUIDING QUESTIONS:

1. How did politics in the United States differ in 1860 from what it had been the 1830s and 1840s?
2. When exactly did this change begin to take place? What appears to be the sequence of events by which this change happened?

DRAWING CONCLUSIONS:

1. What do these election results reveal about the process by which politics in the United States became polarized along North-South lines?

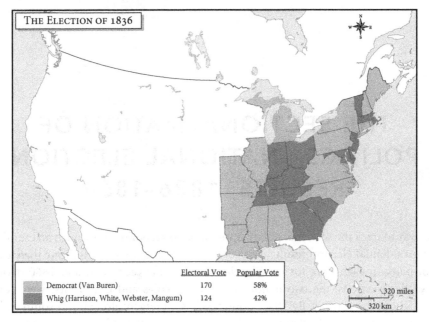

MAP 4. THE ELECTION OF 1836

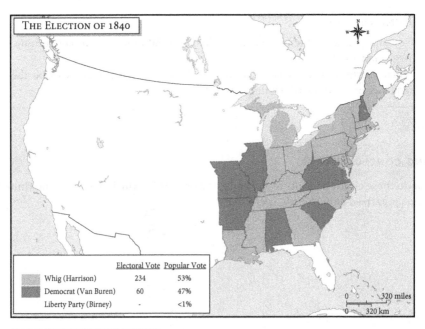

MAP 5. THE ELECTION OF 1840

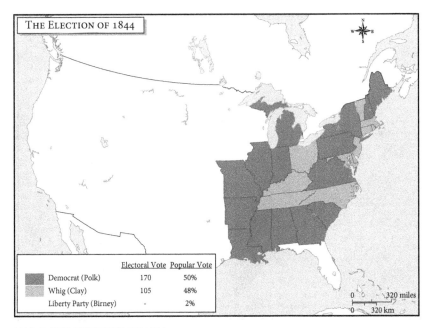

MAP 6. THE ELECTION OF 1844

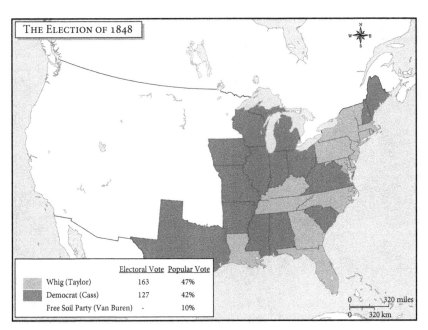

MAP 7. THE ELECTION OF 1848

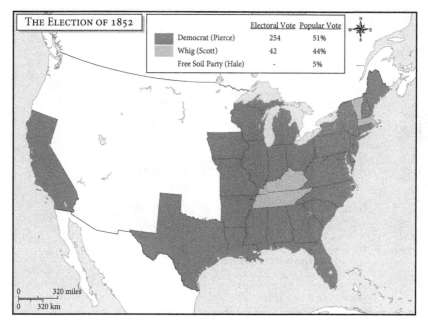

MAP 8. THE ELECTION OF 1852

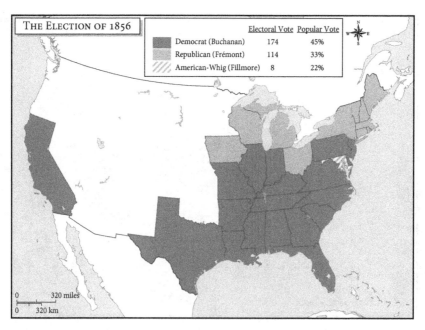

MAP 9. THE ELECTION OF 1856

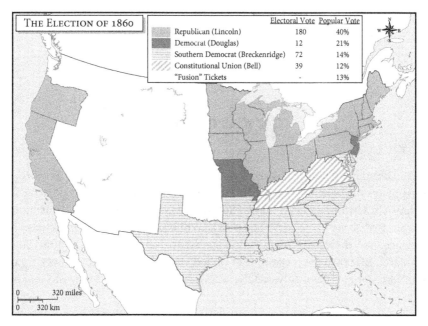

MAP 10. THE ELECTION OF 1860

SECESSION

Between December 1860 and February 1861, seven southern states seceded from the United States of America. The spark for secession was the election of Republican candidate Abraham Lincoln in November 1860 on a free soil platform promising to prevent the expansion of slavery into new territories. While not all white southerners advocated independence, and there were many who vigorously opposed it, by the time Lincoln took office in March of 1861, the secessionists rallied enough support to achieve their goals in seven southern states. What motivated the secession movement and why was that movement successful?

4.1 SECESSION DOCUMENTS

In these documents, we can see the case for secession made in the secessionists' own words. The documents include newspaper editorials from a variety of southern cities. The first of the editorials preceded the November election, though most were published afterward. (One of the newspapers, the New Orleans *Bee*, was at first skeptical of secession but eventually embraced the secessionist position.) Also included are the declarations issued by the South Carolina and Mississippi secession conventions making the case for independence. (South Carolina was the first state to secede.)

GUIDING QUESTION:

1. What reasons do the authors of the documents give for secession? Look for common patterns.

CHARLESTON MERCURY, OCTOBER 11, 1860

A few days since we endeavored to show that the pictures of ruin and desolation to the South, which the submissionists to Black Republican domination were so continually drawing, to "fright us from our propriety," were unreal and false. We propose now to reverse the picture, and to show what will probably be the consequences of a submission of the Southern States, to the rule of Abolitionism at Washington, in the persons of Messrs. LINCOLN and HAMLIN, should they be elected to the Presidency and Vice-Presidency of the United States.

1. The first effect of the submission of the South, to the installation of Abolitionists in the offices of President and Vice-President of the United States, must be a powerful consolidation of the strength of the Abolition party at the North. Success generally strengthens. If, after all, the threats of resistance and disunion, made in Congress and out of Congress, the Southern States sink down into acquiescence, the demoralization of the South will be complete. Add the patronage resulting from the control of ninety-four thousand offices, and the expenditure of eighty

millions of money annually, and they must be irresistible in controlling the Government.

2. To plunder the South for the benefit of the North, by a new Protective Tariff, will be one of their first measures of Northern sectional dominion; and, on the other hand, to exhaust the treasury by sectional schemes of appropriation, will be a congenial policy.

3. Immediate danger will be brought to slavery, in all the Frontier States. When a party is enthroned at Washington, in the Executive and Legislative departments of Government, whose creed it is, to repeal the Fugitive Slave Laws, the *under*-ground railroad, will become an *over*-ground railroad. The tenure of slave property will be felt to be weakened; and the slaves will be sent down to the Cotton States for sale, and the Frontier States *enter on the policy of making themselves Free States*.

4. With the control of the Government of the United States, and an organized and triumphant North to sustain them, the Abolitionists will renew their operations upon the South with increased courage. The thousands in every country, who look up to

Dwight Lowell Dumond, ed., *Southern Editorials on Secession* (New York: The Century Co., 1931), 178–181 power, and make gain out of the future, will come out in support of the Abolition Government. The BROWNLOWS and BOTTS, in the South, will multiply. They will organize; and from being a Union Party, to support an Abolition Government, they will become, like the Government they support, Abolitionists. They will have an Abolition Party in the South, of Southern men. The contests for slavery will no longer be one between the North and the South. It will be in the South, between the people of the South.

5. If, in our present position of power and unitedness, we have the raid of JOHN BROWN—and twenty towns burned down in Texas in one year, by abolitionists—what will be the measures of insurrection and incendiarism, which must follow our notorious and abject prostration to Abolition rule at Washington, with all the patronage of the Federal Government, and a Union organization in the South to support it? Secret conspiracy, and its attendant horrors, with rumors of horrors, will hover over every portion of the South; while, in the language of the Black Republican patriarch—GIDDINGS—they will "laugh at your calamities, and mock when your fear cometh."

6. Already there is uneasiness throughout the South, as to the stability of its institution of slavery. But with a submission to the rule of Abolitionists at Washington, thousands of slaveholders will despair of the institution. While the condition of things in the Frontier States will force their slaves on the markets of the Cotton States, the timid in the Cotton States, will also sell their slaves. The general distrust must affect purchasers. The consequence must be, slave property must be greatly depreciated. We see advertisements for the sale of slaves in some of the Cotton States, for the simple object of getting rid of them; and we know that standing orders for the purchase of slaves in this market have been withdrawn, on account of an anticipated decline of value from the political condition of the country.

7. We suppose, that taking in view all these things, it is not extravagant to estimate, that the submission of the South to the administration of the Federal Government under Messrs. LINCOLN and HAMLIN, must reduce the value of slaves in the South, one hundred dollars each. It is computed that there are four millions, three hundred thousand, slaves in the United States. Here, therefore, is a loss to the Southern people of four hundred and thirty millions of dollars, on their slaves alone. Of course, real estate of all kinds must partake also in the depreciation of slaves.

8. Slave property is the foundation of all property in the South. When security in this is shaken, all other property partakes of its instability. Banks, stocks, bonds, must be influenced. Timid men will sell out and leave the South. Confusion, distrust and pressure must reign.

9. Before Messrs. LINCOLN and HAMLIN can be installed in Washington, as President and Vice-President of the United States, the Southern States can dissolve peaceably (we know what we say) their Union with the North. Mr. LINCOLN and his Abolition cohorts, will have no South to reign over. Their game would be blocked. The foundation of their organization would be taken away; and, left to the tender mercies of a baffled, furious and troubled North, they would be cursed and crushed, as the flagitious cause of the disasters around them. But if we submit, and do not dissolve our union with the North, we make the triumph of our Abolition enemies complete, and enable them to consolidate and wield the power of the North, for our destruction.

10. If the South once submits to the rule of Abolitionists by the General Government, there is, probably, an end of all peaceful separation of the Union. We can only escape the ruin they meditate for the South, by war. Armed with the power of the General Government, and their Organizations at the North, they will have no respect for our courage or energy, and they will use the sword for our subjection. If there is any man in the South who believes that we must separate from the North, we appeal to his humanity, in case Mr. LINCOLN is elected, to dissolve our connection with the North, before the 4th of March next.

11. The ruin of the South, by the emancipation of her slaves, is not like the ruin of any other people. It is not a mere loss of liberty, like the Italians under the BOURBONS. It is not heavy taxation, which must still leave the means of living, or otherwise taxation defeats itself. But it is the loss of liberty, property, home, country—everything that makes life worth having. And this loss will probably take place under circumstances of suffering and horror, unsurpassed

in the history of nations. We must preserve our liberties and institutions, under penalties greater than those which impend over any people in the world.

12. Lastly, we conclude this brief statement of the terrors of submission, by declaring, that in our opinion, they are ten-fold greater even than the supposed terrors of disunion.

NEW ORLEANS BEE, NOVEMBER 8, 1860

The election of ABRAHAM LINCOLN is a fixed fact. The telegraph made known the disastrous result almost before the expiration of the day on which the contest took place. Nor can we say that the event created either marked surprise or consternation. Our citizens had been for some time prepared for intelligence adverse to their hopes. The triumphs of Black Republicanism in Pennsylvania, Ohio and Indiana last month portended too surely the catastrophe in November, to leave more than a feeble hope that by timely and powerful exertion it might be averted, and therefore when the public prints yesterday morning announced a Black Republican victory, they proclaimed what nine-tenths of the community had either openly anticipated or secretly apprehended.

We deem it superfluous at this conjecture to recapitulate the principal causes which have contributed to the defeat of the conservative party. Every one knows that apart from the intrinsic strength of the enemy, its ranks were reinforced by tens of thousands at the North whose sympathies with a national organization had been completely alienated by the protracted, envenomed and most unfortunate quarrel between the rival wings of the Democracy. It is not worthwhile again traveling over the history of that shameful feud, or discussing the question whether the friends of DOUGLAS or of BRECKINRIDGE most deserved censure. Our opinions on the subject have been repeatedly expressed; but in view of a misfortune common to the whole South, it is wholly unnecessary to persist in an irritating and now absolutely useless controversy.

The fact which stares us in the face, and which all of us, Bell, Douglas and Breckinridge men, have to consider, is LINCOLN's election. We have to look at this not as a subject of speculation, but as an event of actual occurrence. LINCOLN is chosen President, and whether with or without the consent and participation of the South, will be inaugurated on the 4th March, 1861. And what is equally to the purpose, LINCOLN has been chosen legally and constitutionally, without either fraud or violence, simply by the suffrages of an enormous majority of the people of the North. Against the manner of his election we do not exactly see what we can allege. It is true he was a sectional candidate; and equally true that with the exception of Missouri, Maryland and, to a slight extent, Kentucky and Virginia, he polled no Southern votes—but as neither the Constitution nor the laws compel a candidate to receive votes in every State, there can be no just ground for resistance or revolutionary movements on that score.

It may be said that the administration of a Black Republican President must necessarily be of an aggressive character towards the South; and that we should forestall so iniquitous a policy by withdrawing from the Union. This view of the subject is fallacious and extremely shallow. In the first place, we have no right to judge of LINCOLN by any thing but his acts, and these can only be appreciated after his inauguration. Secondly, the attempt to break up the Union, before awaiting a single overt act, or even the manifestation of the purpose of the President elect, would be unjustifiable, unprecedented and without the shadow of an excuse. Thirdly, disunion is an uncertain and a perilous remedy, to be invoked only in the last extremity, and as a refuge from wrongs more intolerable than the desperate means by which they are sought to be relieved. Have we yet suffered from such wrongs? Is it not utterly preposterous to pretend that we are cruelly outraged and oppressed? Where is the proof of these allegations? Let the fiery Secessionists adduce these, if they exist, or close their catalogue of fancied woes. Our wrongs are prospective rather than real, nor can they be inflicted so long as ABRAHAM LINCOLN is rendered practically powerless by an adverse Congress.

What we should do may, in our opinion, be summed up in a single word: WAIT. It will be time to fight LINCOLN with gunpowder and the sword, when we find either that constitutional resistance fails, or that he and his party are bent on our humiliation and destruction. We are for the Union so long as it is possible to preserve it. We are willing to go with Louisiana, but every good citizen is bound to use his best efforts to make Louisiana herself go right. A Southern journal—the Newbern (N. C.) *Progress*—in commenting on the probable consequences of LINCOLN's election, remarks:

If Lincoln be elected, of which all good men are fear fully apprehensive, there will be but two parties in the South after the conflict is over—one for union and one for disunion—and then it will be found what were the real objects of those who produced the trouble at Charleston in April last. It is needless for us to say that we shall be found battling for the Union as long as the Federal Government respects the rights of the citizens of North Carolina. Now is the time for all patriotic men to choose positions, for soon they must be found on the one side or the other—for the Union or against it.

We echo that sentiment. Let all patriots choose their position; let them resolve to stand by the Union as long as the Federal Government respects the rights of the citizens of Louisiana. We echo, too, the language of that staunch Democrat, Hon. JOHN S. MILLSON, of Virginia, who, speaking of the election before his constituents at Norfolk, said, "Result as it might, in sixty days after it was over there would be no Bell, Douglas or Breckinridge party in the country. There would be but two—a party for the Union and one against the Union. He had sided, and would battle with the former!" And so will the Douglas and the Bell men, and a considerable proportion of the Breckinridge men. They will cordially sustain the Union so long as the North respects the constitutional rights of the South. Hence we say again, *let us wait!*

NEW ORLEANS BEE, NOVEMBER 28, 1860

We are sorry to remark that in spite of the dearest and most convincing manifestations, the people of the North appear afflicted with transcendental dubiety in respect to the earnestness and reality of Southern movements. The numerous public meetings in the South; the determined expression of hostility to a further political connection with the North; the evidences overwhelming and palpable of high-wrought excitement and invisible resolve—all seem lost upon them. If we are allowed to appreciate Northern feeling on the subject by the tone of its press, we must conclude that a large majority of the people of that section apprehend no serious peril to the Union. It is true they cannot possibly overlook the demonstrations in South Carolina, or deny the avowed succession movements in that State; but they continue to talk of South Carolina as if she were a forward child, to be coaxed or chastised into obedience, while they fancy, in their strange and unaccountable incredulity, that Georgia, and Alabama, and Mississippi, and Florida, and Texas, and Arkansas, and Louisiana are merely laboring under temporary excitement, and have no well defined object in view. There are journals which claim to be better informed respecting the existing phases of Southern feeling. The New York *Herald* and the New York *Express* approximate in their estimates to the true state of the case. But these are only two out of hundreds. Even as able and usually well posted a sheet as the New York *Times* fails fully to comprehend the issue. The *Times* admits that the movement in the South is a popular one—impressive on account of its unanimity and evident sincerity, and important, by reason of its bearing upon the destinies, social and political, of our common country. It acknowledges, too, with some surprise that the movement encounters less opposition than was anticipated, from what it terms "the conservative sentiment of the South." It confesses that the secession feeling appears to have control of the public mind in all the cotton States, and in South Carolina it is unanimous. And yet while conceding all these alarming tendencies, and deducing from them discriminating and just conclusions, the *Times* displays the shallowness of its knowledge by attaching immense importance to the speeches of ALEXANDER H. STEPHENS, and to a few Union meetings recently held in Georgia. This is a signal and striking illustration of the ignorance which pervades the North touching Southern sentiment. Even the more sagacious

Dwight Lowell Dumond, ed., Southern Editorials on Secession (New York: The Century Co., 1931), 274–276.

spirits who see the horizon darken and hear the thunder roll, refuse to admit that the storm is near, because it has not yet burst in violence over the welkin. Others less observant can see nothing more dangerous than a passing cloud, charged, it may be, with a little harmless heat lightning.

We hold it to be a duty of the Southern press, and especially of those papers which are usually deemed conservative, to point out to the North the gross error under which it is laboring. There are two capital and pernicious mistakes in the Northern mind—first, in supposing that the Southern movement is limited in extent, or simply effervescent and fugitive in character; and next, in imagining, as does the *Times*, that a quiescent do-nothing policy by the North will accomplish any good whatever. We, who have ardently loved the Union, who have clung to it persistently, and will still cling to it if we can do so without dishonor, we can assure the North that its ideas of the Southern secession movements are short-sighted and inaccurate. In the first place, this disunion proclivity is an epidemic in everyone of the Cotton States. Those citizens who were once wont to boast their unconditional attachment to the Union have disappeared. If there are any left, they are few in numbers, and indisposed to give free vent to their opinions. The only visible difference of sentiment among the people of the Cotton States regards the timeliness of immediate action. South Carolina raises an unbroken voice for unconditional secession and separate State action. She will go out of the Union as soon as her constituted authorities have made the requisite preparations. Whether accompanied or followed by others, the Palmetto State will secede.

With regard to her sister States, let the people of the North fully understand that their dominant and unalterable position is that the question has to be settled, or the Union will be dissolved. We speak now of those citizens of the South who have generally been considered moderate. There are thousands amongst us who are ripe for a more violent and precipitate remedy, and who would be ready to-morrow to march out of the Union and leave the consequences to GOD. We believe, however, the majority favor joint action by the South; that they desire to see the South assemble in convention, and deliberate and act in common. They are willing, before taking the final step of severance, to give to the North a chance of conciliation; to allow it time for reflection and retrogression. If the North is really anxious to preserve the Union, the entire weight of responsibility is with her. She is the aggressor; we the aggrieved. Her State legislation; her predominant doctrines; her prevailing sentiments; her practical enforcement of a hideous fanaticism, as just evidenced in the election of LINCOLN; her persistent abuse of and assaults upon Southern institutions; her John Brown raids and Montgomery forays—all furnish damning proof that she is the aggressor. Let not the North delude itself with the fallacious impression that anything short of a radical revolution in her policy can or will postpone or avert the calamity of disunion. Let her be assured that the South is not swayed by a temporary gust of passion; that this is no partial movement in opposition to the opinions of the masses like the Nashville Convention of 1850. Woe to the Union if the North still remains blind to the tremendous auguries and portents around her! Woe to it, if having sown the wind, the North fails to see that she is reaping the whirlwind!

There is another point to be considered, and we take occasion to state that in setting forth the views of the South we are simply making known *facts*. There is no remedy for the evils complained of, save an entire change in Northern policy. The South does not look upon the triumph of LINCOLN, *per se*, with any special apprehension, but simply regards it as the crown and capstone of grievance, the last straw on the camel's back, the drop that causes the cup of bitterness to overflow. It denotes the foregone conclusion of the North, and is the entering wedge to the series of hostile measures of which the South will be the victim if she remains within the Union. Hence the solemn and unchangeable determination of her sons to have plenary guarantees of future safety and equality within the Union, or independence out of it. The South stands upon her reserved rights. She proposes nothing; she suggests nothing. It is for the North—if sufficiently impressed with the approaching danger, and solicitous to avert it—to tender justice, and nothing short of justice will content the South.

What we have written respecting Southern sentiment is sober truth, and we trust the North may so accept it. It is as certain as any future event that unless the North is prepared to discard sectionalism in every respect, to repeal its obnoxious laws, to secure to the South the peaceful and unmolested possession of her property, to acknowledge her absolute equality before the Constitution and the laws, the Confederacy of the States will not survive the fourth of March next.

SOUTH CAROLINA'S DECLARATION OF CAUSES, DECEMBER 24, 1860

Declaration of the Immediate Causes Which Induce and Justify the Succession of South Carolina from the Federal Union

The people of the State of South Carolina, in Convention assembled, on the 26th day of April, A.D. 1852, declared that the frequent violations of the Constitution of the United States, by the Federal Government, and its encroachments upon the reserved rights of the States, fully justified this State in then withdrawing from the Federal Union; but in deference to the opinions and wishes of the other slaveholding States, she forbore at that time to exercise this right. Since that time, these encroachments have continued to increase, and further forbearance ceases to be a virtue.

And now the State of South Carolina having resumed her separate and equal place among nations, deems it due to herself, to the remaining United States of America, and to the nations of the world, that she should declare the immediate causes which have led to this act.

In the year 1765, that portion of the British Empire embracing Great Britain, undertook to make laws for the government of that portion composed of the thirteen American Colonies. A struggle for the right of self-government ensued, which resulted, on the 4th of July, 1776, in a Declaration, by the Colonies, "that they are, and of right out to be, FREE AND INDEPENDENT STATES; and that, as free and independent States, they have full power to levy war, conclude peace, contract alliances, establish commerce, and to do all other acts and things which independent States may of right do."

They further solemnly declared that whenever any "form of government becomes destructive of the ends for which it was established, it is the right of the people to alter or abolish it, and to institute a new government." Deeming the Government of Great Britain to have become destructive of these ends, they declared that the Colonies "are absolved from all allegiance to the British Crown, and that all political connection between them and the State of Great Britain is, and out to be, totally dissolved."

In pursuance of this Declaration of Independence, each of the thirteen States proceeded to exercise its separate sovereignty; adopted for itself a Constitution, and appointed officers for the administration of government in all its departments—Legislative, Executive and Judicial. For purposes of defense, they united their arms and their counsels; and, in 1778, they entered into a League known as the Articles of Confederation, whereby they agreed to entrust the administration of their external relations to a common agent, known as the Congress of the United States, expressly declaring, in the first Article "that each State retains its sovereignty, freedom and independence, and every power, jurisdiction and right which is not, by this Confederation, expressly delegated to the United States in Congress assembled."

Under this Confederation the war of the Revolution was carried on, and on the 3rd of September, 1783, the contest ended, and a definite Treaty was signed by Great Britain, in which she acknowledged the independence of the Colonies in the following terms:

"ARTICLE 1—His Britannic Majesty acknowledges the said United States, viz: new Hampshire, Massachusetts Bay, Rhode Island and Providence Plantations, Connecticut, New York, New Jersey, Pennsylvania, Delaware, Maryland, Virginia, North Carolina, South Carolina and Georgia, to be FREE, SOVEREIGN AND

Declaration of the Immediate Causes Which Induce and Justify the Succession of South Carolina from the Federal Union (Charleston: Evans and Cogswell, (1860), 3–10.

INDEPENDENT STATES; that he treats them as such; and for himself, his heirs and successors, relinquishes all claims to the government, property and territorial rights of the same and every part thereof."

Thus were established the two great principles asserted by the Colonies, namely: the right of a State to govern itself; and the right of a people to abolish a Government when it becomes destructive of the ends for which it was instituted. And concurrent with the established of these principles, was the fact, that each Colony became and was recognized by the mother Country a FREE, SOVEREIGN AND INDEPENDENT STATE.

In 1787, Deputies were appointed by the States to revise the Articles of Confederation, and on 17th September, 1787, these Deputies were recommended for the adoption of the States, the Articles of Union, known as the Constitution of the United States.

The parties to whom this Constitution was submitted, were the several sovereign States; they were to agree or disagree, and when nine of them agreed the compact was to take effect among those concurring, and the General Government, as the common agent, was then invested with their authority.

If only nine of the thirteen States had concurred, the other four would have remained as they then were—separate, sovereign States, independent of any of the provisions of the Constitution. In fact, two of the States did not accede the Constitution until long after it had gone into operation among the other eleven; and during that interval, they each exercised the functions of an independent nation.

By this Constitution, certain duties were imposed upon the several States, and the exercise of certain of their powers was restrained, which necessarily implied their continued existence as sovereign States. But to remove all doubt, an amendment was added, which declared that the powers not delegated to the United States by the Constitution, nor prohibited by it to the States, are reserved to the States, respectively, or to the people. On the 23rd May, 1788, South Carolina, by a Convention of her People, passed an Ordinance assenting to this Constitution, and afterwards altered her own Constitution, to conform herself to the obligations she had undertaken.

Thus was established, by compact between the States, a Government with definite objects and powers,

limited to the express words of the grant. This limitation left the whole remaining mass of power subject to the clause reserving it to the States or to the people, and rendered unnecessary any specification of reserved rights.

We hold that the Government thus established is subject to the two great principles asserted in the Declaration of Independence; and we hold further, that the mode of its formation subjects it to a third fundamental principle, namely: the law of compact. We maintain that in every compact between two or more parties, the obligation is mutual; that the failure of one of the contracting parties to perform a material part of the agreement, entirely releases the obligation of the other; and that where no arbiter is provided, each part is remitted to his own judgement to determine the fact of failure, with all its consequences.

In the present case, that fact is established with certainty. We assert that fourteen of the States have deliberately refused, for years past, to fulfill their constitutional obligations, and we refer to their own States for proof.

The Constitution of the United States, in its fourth Article, provides as follows:

"No person held to service or labor in one state, under the laws thereof, escaping into another, shall, in consequence of any law or regulation therein, be discharged from such service or labor, but shall be delivered up on claim of the party to whom such service or labor may be due."

This stipulation was so material to the compact,that without it that compact would not have been made. The greater number of the contracting parties held slaves, and they had previously evinced their estimate of the value of such a stipulation by making it a condition in the Ordinance for the government of the territory ceded by Virginia, which now composes the States north of the Ohio River.

The same article of the Constitution stipulates also for rendition by the several States of fugitives from justice from the other States.

The General Government, as the common agent, passed laws to carry into effect these stipulations of the States. For many years these laws were executed. But an increasing hostility on the part of the non-slaveholding States to the institution of slavery, has led to a disregard of their obligations, and the laws of the General Government have ceased to effect the objects of the Constitution. The States of Maine, New Hampshire, Vermont, Massachusetts, Connecticut, Rhode Island, New York, Pennsylvania, Illinois, Indiana, Michigan, Wisconsin and Iowa, have enacted laws which either nullify the Acts of Congress or render useless any attempt to execute them. In many of these States the fugitive is discharged from service or labor claimed, and in none of them has the State Government complied with the stipulation made in the Constitution. The State of New Jersey, at an early day, passed a law in conformity with her constitutional obligation; but the current of anti-slavery feeling has led her more recently to enact laws which render inoperative the remedies provided by her own law and by the laws of Congress. In the State of New York even the right of transit for a slave has been denied by her tribunals; and the States of Ohio and Iowa have refused to surrender to justice fugitives charged with murder, and with inciting servile insurrection in the State of Virginia. Thus the constituted compact has been deliberately broken and disregarded by the non-slaveholding States, and the consequence follows that South Carolina is released from her obligation.

The ends for which the Constitution was framed are declared by itself to be "to form a more perfect union, establish justice, insure domestic tranquility, provide for the common defence, promote the general welfare, and secure the blessings of liberty to ourselves and our posterity."

These ends it endeavored to accomplish by a Federal Government, in which each State was recognized as an equal, and had separate control over its own institutions. The right of property in slaves was recognized by giving to free persons distinct political rights, by giving them the right to represent, and burthening them with direct taxes for three-fifths of their slaves; by authorizing the importation of slaves for twenty years; and by stipulating for the rendition of fugitives from labor.

We affirm that these ends for which this Government was instituted have been defeated, and the Government itself has been made destructive of them by the action of the non-slaveholding States.

Those States have assume the right of deciding upon the propriety of our domestic institutions; and have denied the rights of property established in fifteen of the States and recognized by the Constitution; they have denounced as sinful the institution of slavery; they have permitted open establishment among them of societies, whose avowed object is to disturb the peace and to eloign the property of the citizens of other States. They have encouraged and assisted thousands of our slaves to leave their homes; and those who remain, have been incited by emissaries, books and pictures to servile insurrection.

For twenty-five years this agitation has been steadily increasing, until it has now secured to its aid the power of the common Government. Observing the *forms* of the Constitution, a sectional party has found within that Article establishing the Executive Department, the means of subverting the Constitution itself. A geographical line has been drawn across the Union, and all the States north of that line have united in the election of a man to the high office of President of the United States, whose opinions and purposes are hostile to slavery. He is to be entrusted with the administration of the common Government, because he has declared that that "Government cannot endure permanently half slave, half free," and that the public mind must rest in the belief that slavery is in the course of ultimate extinction.

This sectional combination for the submersion of the Constitution, has been aided in some of the States by elevating to citizenship, persons who, by the supreme law of the land, are incapable of becoming citizens; and their votes have been used to inaugurate a new policy, hostile to the South, and destructive of its beliefs and safety.

On the 4th day of March next, this party will take possession of the Government. It has announced that the South shall be excluded from the common territory, that the judicial tribunals shall be made sectional, and that a war must be waged against slavery until it shall cease throughout the United States.

The guaranties of the Constitution will then no longer exist; the equal rights of the States will be lost. The slaveholding States will no longer have the power of self-government, or self-protection, and the Federal Government will have become their enemy.

Sectional interest and animosity will deepen the irritation, and all hope of remedy is rendered vain, by the fact that public opinion at the North has invested a great political error with the sanction of more erroneous religious belief.

We, therefore, the People of South Carolina, by our delegates in Convention assembled, appealing to the Supreme Judge of the world for the rectitude of our intentions, have solemnly declared that the Union heretofore existing between this State and the other States of North America, is dissolved, and that the State of South Carolina has resumed her position among the nations of the world, as a separate and independent State; with full power to levy war, conclude peace, contract alliances, establish commerce, and to do all other acts and things which independent States may of right do.

Adopted December 24, 1860

MISSISSIPPI'S DECLARATION OF CAUSES, JANUARY 26, 1861

A DECLARATION OF THE IMMEDIATE CAUSES WHICH INDUCE AND JUSTIFY THE SECESSION OF THE STATE OF MISSISSIPPI FROM THE FEDERAL UNION

In the momentous step which our State has taken of dissolving its connection with the government of which we so long formed a part, it is but just that we should declare the prominent reasons which have induced our course.

Our position is thoroughly identified with the institution of slavery—the greatest material interest of the world. Its labor supplies the product which constitutes by far the largest and most important portions of commerce of the earth. These products are peculiar to the climate verging on the tropical regions, and by an imperious law of nature, none but the black race can bear exposure to the tropical sun. These products have become necessities of the world, and a blow at slavery is a blow at commerce and civilization.

That blow has been long aimed at the institution, and was at the point of reaching its consummation. There was no choice left us but submission to the mandates of abolition, or a dissolution of the Union, whose principles had been subverted to work out our ruin.

That we do not overstate the dangers to our institution, a reference to a few facts will sufficiently prove.

The hostility to this institution commenced before the adoption of the Constitution, and was manifested in the well-known Ordinance of 1787, in regard to the Northwestern Territory.

The feeling increased, until, in 1819–20, it deprived the South of more than half the vast territory acquired from France.

The same hostility dismembered Texas and seized upon all the territory acquired from Mexico.

It has grown until it denies the right of property in slaves, and refuses protection to that right on the high seas, in the Territories, and wherever the government of the United States had jurisdiction.

It refuses the admission of new slave States into the Union, and seeks to extinguish it by confining it within its present limits, denying the power of expansion.

It tramples the original equality of the South under foot.

It has nullified the Fugitive Slave Law in almost every free State in the Union, and has utterly broken the compact which our fathers pledged their faith to maintain.

It advocates negro equality, socially and politically, and promotes insurrection and incendiarism in our midst.

It has enlisted its press, its pulpit and its schools against us, until the whole popular mind of the North is excited and inflamed with prejudice.

It has made combinations and formed associations to carry out its schemes of emancipation in the States and wherever else slavery exists.

It seeks not to elevate or to support the slave, but to destroy his present condition without providing a better.

From *A Declaration of the Immediate Causes which Induce and Justify the Secession of the State of Mississippi from the Federal Union* (Jackson: Mississippian Book and Job Printing Office, 1861), 3–5.

It has invaded a State, and invested with the honors of martyrdom the wretch whose purpose was to apply flames to our dwellings, and the weapons of destruction to our lives.

It has broken every compact into which it has entered for our security.

It has given indubitable evidence of its design to ruin our agriculture, to prostrate our industrial pursuits and to destroy our social system.

It knows no relenting or hesitation in its purposes; it stops not in its march of aggression, and leaves us no room to hope for cessation or for pause.

It has recently obtained control of the Government, by the prosecution of its unhallowed schemes, and destroyed the last expectation of living together in friendship and brotherhood.

Utter subjugation awaits us in the Union, if we should consent longer to remain in it. It is not a matter of choice, but of necessity. We must either submit to degradation, and to the loss of property worth four billions of money, or we must secede from the Union framed by our fathers, to secure this as well as every other species of property. For far less cause than this, our fathers separated from the Crown of England.

Our decision is made. We follow their footsteps. We embrace the alternative of separation; and for the reasons here stated, we resolve to maintain our rights with the full consciousness of the justice of our course, and the undoubting belief of our ability to maintain it.

DRAWING CONCLUSION:

1. What reasons do these documents give for secession? What does this reveal about the reasons that Lincoln's election led to the secession of seven southern states?

CASE STUDY—THE SECESSION OF GEORGIA

With the exception of South Carolina, where the move to declare independence happened quickly and with relatively little dissent, in every other southern state there was a vigorous debate over the merits of secession. A deeper examination of the secession debate in one particular state, Georgia, can shed light on the arguments of the secessionists and the reasons why their arguments eventually carried the day.

Secession in Georgia took place through a two-step process. Shortly after Lincoln's election, the state legislature began to debate the issue of secession. At issue was a proposal to hold a special state convention that would determine whether or not Georgia would declare independence. After about a week of debate, the legislature approved legislation to hold a secession convention. An election for delegates to the convention was held the first week of January 1861. A narrow majority of votes were cast for candidates who were in support of Georgia's immediate secession. The convention convened on January 16; and three days later, by a vote of 166–130, the delegates declared Georgia's independence.

The secession issue was hotly debated both within the legislature and in the campaign for convention delegates. The tenor of the debate within the legislature and out on the campaign trail, though, differed somewhat. Georgia's legislature tended to be dominated by wealthy politicians with direct ties to the plantation economy. The legislative debates can therefore be thought of as a place where members of Georgia's economic and political elite discussed how best to respond to Lincoln's election. Once the state's political leaders decided in favor secession, however, the policy still had to be sold to the broader electorate, most of whom were not slave owners. (In 1860, 63% of white Georgians were members of families that owned no slaves.) Examining Georgia's two-step secession process thus allows us to explore both how the state's economic and political elite discussed the issue among themselves and how secession was sold to non-slave owners.

5.1   A TIMELINE OF GEORGIA'S SECESSION

- November 6, 1860—Abraham Lincoln elected President of the United States.
- November 12—The Georgia state legislature begins debating the issue of secession.
- November 20—The legislature approves a bill to hold a special state convention to consider a secession ordinance.
- January 2, 1861—Election held to choose delegates to the state secession convention.
- January 16—The state secession convention convenes.
- January 19—Convention delegates approve a secession ordinance declaring Georgia's independence from the United States.

5.2 THOMAS R.R. COBB'S SECESSIONIST SPEECH, NOVEMBER 12, 1860

Georgia's legislature, meeting in the town of Milledgeville, began to consider the issue of emancipation on Monday, November 12, 1860. That evening, Thomas R.R. Cobb, a member of one of Georgia's leading political families, delivered a public address in which he made a passionate case for the necessity of secession. The speech can be divided into two sections. In the first part, Cobb argues for the legality of secession. (There were others who took the position that states had no constitutional right to secede from the Union.) Having established the case of the legality of secession, Cobb then shifts gears to make the case for the necessity of secession. Pay particular attention to this second part of the speech, where he argues for the political necessity of secession. What does Cobb warn will happen if Georgia remains within the Union?

GUIDING QUESTION:

1. On what grounds does Cobb argue that Georgia's secession is a political necessity? What does he warn will happen if Georgia does not secede?

THOMAS R. R. COBB'S SECESSIONIST SPEECH

NOVEMBER 12, 1860

(Excerpts)

I come now to consider this question in its *political* light, and it rises in importance much above the mere legal question.

I must confess that the mere election of a candidate to the Presidency, in a manner legally unconstitutional, does not in my judgement justify necessarily a dissolution of the Union. The wise man and the statesman, to say nothing of the patriot, will always weigh well whether "it is better to bear the ills we have than fly to others that we know not of." And, hence, arises the *political* question, does this election justify and require a disruption of the ties which bind us to the Union? As much as I would dislike the triumph of a purely sectional candidate upon a purely sectional platform, I am free to say I should hesitate even then to risk the consequences of a dissolution, provided that sectional platform *was upon issues not vital in themselves, or were temporary in their nature.* Such, would I conceive to be protective tariffs and homestead bills—the acquisition of territory—peace or war with foreign powers. And if the election of Lincoln, unconstitutional though it may be, was upon a temporary issue, or a question not vital in importance, I should hesitate to declare it ground for Disunion. But my countrymen, I cannot so view the triumph of Black Republicanism. It is a question vital in itself, and by no means, of a temporary character. To see it in its breadth and enormity, to see its dangerous proportions and its threatening aspects, it becomes necessary for us to go back a little in history, and to trace the slavery agitation as connected with our Government. Shortly after its organization, we find a petition from the Quakers of Philadelphia, asking the abolition of slavery. We see that petition treated by an unanimous Congress as the mere ebullition of religious fanaticism, and as it is laid on the

From William W. Freehling and Craig G. Simpson, eds. *Secession Debated: Georgia's Showdown in 1860* (New York: Oxford University Press, 1992), 15–24.

table, we smile at the folly of the broadbrim followers of Fox. In a few years we find petitions accumulating from other Sects and Societies, until, finally, by an overwhelming majority, we find the House of Representatives refusing longer to listen to their fanatical ravings, and as the 21st Rule is adopted, we fondly dreamed that the cockatrice's egg would never be hatched. In a few years we find the floor of Congress desecrated by the ravings of Giddings and other abolitionists, and at the same time, in the Presidential contest, an abolition candidate is presented to the people of the North. But the Abolitionists in Congress are hissed at their ravings, and the miserable handful at the ballot-box only manifested their weakness, and we rested secure in our confidence in the protection of the Constitution.

But a few years more found the miserable demagogues and political leaders of the North, in their party excitement, bidding for this Abolition vote. Without real sympathy for the movement, we find them vieing with each other in pretended zeal, until shortly we find the 21st Rule falling as a sacrifice before the demands of the fanatics. We find the parties in power more and more undecided in denouncing the treason, until finally the great Whig party fell, demoralized, and at the North very much Abolitionized. We find church organizations, and great benevolent institutions, one after another, sundered and divided by the demon, which, once aroused, there was no power to allay. We find reason and argument unheeded, the obligations of oaths and compacts disregarded, the very religion of God desecrated. His Bible denounced, His churches and pulpits polluted, and His children excluded from the communion table of their Master. And then, for the first time, we awake to the great fact that our lives and liberty are in jeopardy unless great exertions for our safety are made. In the meantime, our slaves are stolen, the old remedies are proved useless, new provisions are demanded. The Post Offices become the vehicles for spreading insurrection, and new restrictions are required. Greater demands are made in Congress, and States rejected from the Union because Slavery is recognized by their Constitutions. Finally, the Slave Trade in the District of Columbia is attacked, and the Inter-State Slave Trade. The Wilmot Proviso is placed on all territory, and the South aroused to her danger, demands security and peace. We all remember the great Compromise measures of 1850. They were declared a finality, and the syren song of peace was sung in our ears. Some of us believed it, and we once more laid down in ease. Soon, however, a new question is raised, the monster shows himself again in the Halls of Congress, and once more we hear that the Union is saved and peace restored by the provisions of the Kansas-Nebraska Act. The other events are known to you. This Black Republican party is formed; Frémont is its candidate; let us crush it now, and the Slavery issue is dead forever. Such was the song. Great exertions are made. Frémont is defeated, and we hope on for peace. There seems to be a lull in the storm. One of Georgia's distinguished sons voluntarily terminates his long public career, and as he bids farewell to his constituents, he informs us in a public address (honestly, I have no doubt), that the battle is over, the victory won, that he lays off his armor because there is no other foe to meet, and he shows to our willing ears what great things had been done for us, "whereof we were glad." But hardly had he reached his quiet home, ere the territory of Virginia is invaded by a lawless band under John Brown, and today you find him with his armor again buckled on, to re-save the Union once more—to re-deliver us from the fanatical devil. And now, after four years of argument and persuasion, and entreaty and remonstrance and warning, tonight, my friends, we find this demon master of our strongholds, this party, so long to be destroyed, more rampant and more triumphant than ever—with almost fabulous majorities in every Northern State—placing in the Executive Chair one of the most objectionable and fanatical of its leaders. Are we blind, that this retrospect shall teach us no lesson? Read upon the banners of this army, and see what are its objects and aims: "*No more Slave States;*" "*The Repeal of the Fugitive Slave Law;*" "*Relief from the Slave Power;*" "*The Irrepressible Conflict;*" "*No League with Hell.*" Look at its leaders, and see the heroes who deify John Brown; the mad preachers, like Cheever and Beecher; the Fourierites, led by Greely; the Sewards and Sumners, and Hales and Fred Douglas [sic]. Look at its cohorts, and see their mottled ranks—free negroes and boot-blacks, coachmen and domestics, infidels and free-lovers, spiritual rappers and every other shade of mania and folly. Search in vain among them all, for one gentleman like Everett, one sound conservative like Fillmore, one bold statesman like Cushing or O'Connor, one noble patriot like Buchanan, one daring leader like Douglas. Scan closely all its long list of speakers or voters as far as we can see them, and where is the man you would ask into your table, or with whose arm you would walk through the streets. And yet these are our rulers. To them we are called to submit. Let me rather have a king, for I can respect him; or an emperor, for I may cajole him; or an aristocracy, for they will not envy, and dare not hate me. Nay, let me die before I shall bow before such fanatics as these.

The question, then, is vital. Is it temporary? The history of its insignificant rise and rapid progress—the little cloud, no bigger than a man's hand, which has now overspread the whole heavens—the thunders which we hear too distinctly to be misunderstood—the insolence which even the prospect of power has given to craven cowards—that already they taunt us with timidity and threaten us with chastisement—aye, a hundred indications too plain to be mistaken, say to everything but stolid ignorance or blind fatuity, that this is but "the beginning of the end." My friends, history and philosophy would have informed us years ago of the same truth, had we listened to their teachings. Fanaticism is madness, is insanity. It has a zeal laudable in its earnestness, admirable in its honesty. Its error is in the false foundation on which it builds. Its danger lies in the depth of its convictions, which will not allow it to attend to reason, but makes it as "'the deaf adder which will not listen to the charmers, charming never so wisely." Its fountain lies deep in the human heart. Its bonds are interwoven with many of the noblest principles of our nature. Hence, it ignores consequences, it overrides obstacles, it ruthlessly sunders the dearest ties of the heart, it takes affection from the lover, yea, it steels the mother against her own offspring, the creature against his God. We call it blind, because it cannot see; we call it deaf, because it cannot hear; we call it foolish, because it cannot reason; we call it cruel, because it cannot feel. By what channel, then, can you reach its citadel? Firmly planted therein, with every

avenue closed to ingress, and yet every door of evil influence open to the bitter issues which flow without, the deluded victim glories in his own shame, and scatters ruin and destruction, in the mad dream that he is doing God's service. Such is the teaching of philosophy, and history, her handmaid, confirms its truth. The bloody minds of those who, with sinful hands, murdered the Lord of Glory, were never sated until the Roman legions sacked the city of David, and the Eagle of Rome floated over the ruins of the Temple. The fires of Smithfield never ceased to burn until the maiden Queen, with her strong arm and stronger will, sealed in the blood of Mary, the covenant of peace to the Church. The wheel of the Juggernaut never failed to crush the bones of infatuated victims, until the shaggy mane of the British Lion was drenched in the blood of Oriental imbecility. The bloody Crescent of the false prophet never ceased to behold the gory victims which Islam claimed, until on many a battlefield the redemption in blood came to rescue the children of Faith. The Ganges bore in its turbid waters the innocent victims to the delusion of mothers, until Britain assumed the position which God held to Abraham on the Mount, and staying the murderous arms, bade the well-spring of a mother's love once more to gush from a mother's heart. Why should I continue the review? All history speaks but one voice. Tell me when and where the craving appetite of fanaticism was ever gorged with victims; when and where its bloody hands were ever stayed by the consciousness of satiety; when and where its deaf ears ever listened to reason, or argument, or persuasion, or selfishness; when and where it ever died from fatigue, or yielded except in blood. When you have done this, you may then convince me that this is a temporary triumph, and bid me hope on. Till you do this, I must listen to the teachings of reason, philosophy and history, and believe that Lincoln and Seward spoke the truth when they said, this contest is never ended until all these States are either free or slave.

Mark me, my friends. The only tie which binds together this party at the North is the Slavery issue. Bank and Anti-Bank, Protection and Free Trade, Old Whig and Old Democrat, have all come together. The old issues are ignored, forgotten. Abolitionism and Agrarianism are the only specialties in their platform. This Aaron's rod has swallowed up all the others, and upon it alone has the battle been fought and the victory won. And no man and no party can make terms or obtain quarter from these fanatics, except by bowing down and worshipping this Moloch. Even in this election, have not the Southern parties offered candidates on every shade of opinion, to this Northern horde, and have they not all been rejected with scorn? Did not Bell and Douglas and Breckenridge, one or the other, agree with them on every question except Slavery? Why were they rejected? Herculean efforts have been made. Argument and eloquence have been offered lavishly, and money almost as lavishly, to bid off and buy up this motley crew. Scorn, contempt, insolence and contumely have been the only answer we have received. Can any man shut his eyes and still cry the syren song, "Hope on. Hope on?"

We have seen, then, that this election is legally unconstitutional, and that politically the issue on which it is unconstitutional is both vital in its importance and permanent in its effects. What, then, is our remedy? Shall it be the boy's redress of recrimination? the bully's redress of braggadocio or boasting? or the manly freeman's redress of Independence? This is a most solemn question, and no man should rashly advise his countrymen at such a time. For myself, for months, nay years, I have foreseen this coming cloud. I have given it all the study of which my mind is possessed. I have called my heart into the council and listened to its beatings. Nay, more, my friends, I fear not to say I have gone to the God I worship, and begged him to advise me. On the night of the 6th of November, I called my wife and little ones together around my family altar, and together we prayed to God to stay the wrath of our oppressors, and preserve the Union of our fathers. The rising sun of the seventh of November found me on my knees, begging the same kind Father to make that wrath to praise Him, and the remainder of wrath to restrain. I believe that the hearts of men are in His hands, and when the telegraph announced to me that the voice of the North proclaimed at the ballot-box that I should be a slave, I heard in the same sound, the voice of my God speaking through His Providence, and saying to His child, "Be free! Be free!"

Marvel not then that I say my voice is for immediate, unconditional secession.

DRAWING CONCLUSION:

1. What is Cobb's argument for the necessity of Georgia's secession? What does he warn will happen if Georgia does not secede? What does this reveal about the reasons that secessionists like Cobb favored independence?

5.3 ALEXANDER STEPHENS' UNIONIST SPEECH, NOVEMBER 14, 1860

On November 14, Alexander Stephens, perhaps the state's most prominent Unionist, delivered a public address in Milledgeville in which he countered the arguments of Thomas R. R. Cobb and other secessionists. Stephens had a distinguished political career, including sixteen years of service in the United States House of Representatives, where he had met and established a friendship with Abraham Lincoln, a little-known Congressman from Illinois. Stephens retired from politics in 1859, but he became increasingly outspoken in his criticisms of those he considered southern extremists. Although Stephens's November 14th speech was widely hailed as a triumph, in the end, his efforts to keep Georgia in the Union were unsuccessful. Following Georgia's January 1861 declaration of independence, Stephens renounced his loyalty to the United States and shortly thereafter was selected to serve as Vice President of the Confederacy. As you read Stephens's speech, pay attention both to his argument for the Union as well as the points that he concedes to secessionists like Cobb.

GUIDING QUESTIONS:

1. What is Stephens's argument against secession? What does he warn will happen if Georgia secedes?
2. What points does Stephens concede to the secessionists? On what points do he and Cobb agree?

ALEXANDER STEPHENS'S UNIONIST SPEECH

NOVEMBER 14, 1860

(Excerpts)

The first question that presents itself is, shall the people of the South secede from the Union in consequence of the election of Mr. Lincoln to the Presidency of the United States? My countrymen, I tell you frankly, candidly, and earnestly, that I do not think that they ought. In my judgment, the election of no man, constitutionally chosen to that high office, is sufficient cause for any State to separate from the Union. It ought to stand by and aid still in maintaining the constitution of the country. To make a point of resistance to the government, to withdraw from it because a man has been constitutionally elected, puts us in the wrong. We are pledged to maintain the constitution. Many of us have sworn to support it. Can we,

therefore, for the mere election of a man to the presidency, and that, too, in accordance with the prescribed forms of the constitution, make a point of resistance to the government, without becoming the breakers of that sacred instrument ourselves, by withdrawing ourselves from it? Would we not be in the wrong? Whatever fate is to befall this country, let it never be laid to the charge of the people of the South, and especially to the people of Georgia, that we were untrue to our national engagements. Let the fault and the wrong rest upon others. If all our hopes are to be blasted, if the republic is to go down, let us be found to the last moment standing on the deck with the constitution of the United States waving over our heads. Let the fanatics of the North break the constitution, if such is their fell purpose. Let the responsibility be upon them. I shall speak presently more of their acts; but let not the South, let us not be the ones to commit the aggression.

William W. Freehling and Craig M. Simpson, eds., *Secession Debated: Georgia's Showdown in 1860* (New York: Oxford University Press, 1992), 55–59, 63, 67–70, 78–79.

We went into the election with this people. The result was different from what we wished; but the election has been constitutionally held. Were we to make a point of resistance to the government and go out of the Union on that account, the record would be made up hereafter against us.

But it is said Mr. Lincoln's policy and principles are against the constitution, and that, if he carries them out, it will be destructive of our rights. Let us not anticipate a threatened evil. If he violates the constitution, then will come our time to act. Do not let us break it because, forsooth, he may. If he does, that is the time for us to strike. I think it would be injudicious and unwise to do this sooner. I do not anticipate that Mr. Lincoln will do anything to jeopard[ize] our safety or security, whatever may be his spirit to do it; for he is bound by the constitutional checks which are thrown around him, which at this time render him powerless to do any great mischief. This shows the wisdom of our system. The President of the United States is no emperor, no dictator—he is clothed with no absolute power. He can do nothing unless he is backed by power in Congress. The House of Representatives is largely in a majority against him. In the very face and teeth of the heavy majority which he has obtained in the northern States, there have been large gains in the House of Representatives to the conservative constitutional party of the country, which here I will call the national democratic party, because that is the cognomen it has at the North. There are twelve of this party elected from New York to the next Congress, I believe. In the present House there are but four, I think. In Pennsylvania, New Jersey, Ohio, and Indiana, there have been gains. In the present Congress, there were one hundred and thirteen republicans, when it takes one hundred and seventeen to make a majority. The gains in the democratic party in Pennsylvania, Ohio, New Jersey, New York, Indiana, and other States, notwithstanding its distractions, have been enough to make a majority of near thirty in the next House against Mr. Lincoln. Even in Boston, Mr. Burlingame, one of the noted leaders of the fanatics of that section, has been defeated, and a conservative man returned in his stead. Is this the time, then, to apprehend that Mr. Lincoln, with this large majority in the House of Representatives against him, can carry out any of his unconstitutional principles in that body?

In the Senate he will also be powerless. There will be a majority of four against him. This, after the loss of Bigler, Fitch, and others, by the unfortunate dissensions of the national democratic party in their States. Mr. Lincoln cannot appoint an officer without the consent of the Senate—he cannot form a cabinet without the same consent. He will be in the condition of George the Third (the embodiment of Toryism), who had to ask the Whigs to appoint his ministers, and was compelled to receive a cabinet utterly opposed to his views; and so Mr. Lincoln will be compelled to ask of the Senate to choose for him a cabinet, if the democracy of that party chose to put him on such terms. He will be compelled to do this, or let the government stop, if the national democratic men—the conservative men in the Senate—should so determine. Then how can Mr. Lincoln obtain a cabinet which would aid him, or allow him to violate the Constitution[?] Why then, I say, should we disrupt the ties of this Union when his hands are tied—when he can do nothing against us?

I have heard it mooted that no man in the State of Georgia, who is true to her interests, could hold office under Mr. Lincoln. But I ask who appoints to office? Not the President alone; the Senate has to concur. No man can be appointed without the consent of the Senate. Should any man, then, refuse to hold office that was given him by a Democratic Senate?

(Mr. Toombs interrupted, and said, if the Senate was Democratic, it was for Breckinridge.)

Well, then (continued Mr. Stephens), I apprehend that no man could be justly considered untrue to the interests of Georgia, or incur any disgrace, if the interests of Georgia required it, to hold an office which a Breckinridge Senate had given him, even though Mr. Lincoln should be President. (Applause.)

I trust, my countrymen, you will be still and silent. I am addressing your good sense. I am giving you my views in a calm and dispassionate manner, and if any of you differ with me, you can on some other occasion give your views, as I am doing now, and let reason and true patriotism decide between us. In my judgment, I say, under such circumstances, there would be no possible disgrace for a southern man to hold office. No man will be suffered to be appointed, I have no doubt, who is not true to the constitution, if southern senators are true to their trusts, as I cannot permit myself to doubt that they will be.

My honorable friend who addressed you last night (Mr. Toombs), and to whom I listened with the profoundest attention, asks if we would submit to Black Republican rule? I say to you and to him, as a Georgian, I never would submit to any Black Republican aggression upon our Constitutional rights.

I will never myself consent, as much as I admire this Union, for the glories of the past or the blessings of the present, as much as it has done for civilization; as much as the hopes of the world hang upon it; I would never submit to aggression upon my rights to maintain it longer; and if they cannot be maintained in the Union standing on the Georgia platform, where I have stood from the time of its adoption, I would be in favor of disrupting every tie which binds the States together. I will have equality for Georgia, and for the citizens of Georgia, in this Union, or I will look for new safeguards elsewhere. This is my position. The only question now is, can this be secured in the Union? That is what I am counselling with you to-night about. Can it be secured? In my judgment, it may be, but it may not be; but let us do all we can, so that in the future, if the worst comes, it may never be said we were negligent in doing our duty to the last.

My countrymen, I am not of those who believe this Union has been a curse up to this time. True men, men of integrity, entertain different views from me on this subject. I do not question their right to do so; I would not impugn their motives in so doing. Nor will I undertake to say that this government of our fathers is perfect. There is nothing perfect in this world of human origin; nothing connected with human nature, from man himself to any of his works. You may select the wisest and best men for your judges, and yet how many defects are there in the administration of justice? You may select the wisest and best men for your legislators, and yet how many defects are apparent in your laws? And it is so in our government. But that this government of our fathers, with all its defects, comes nearer the objects of all good governments than any other on the face of the earth, is my settled conviction. Contrast it now with any on the face of the earth.

. . .

These, then, were the three grievances or grounds of complaint against the general system of our government and its workings; I mean the administration of the Federal government. As to the acts of several of the States, I shall speak presently, but these three were the main ones urged against the common head. Now suppose it be admitted that all of these are evils in the system; do they over balance and outweigh the advantages and great good which this same government affords in a thousand innumerable ways that cannot be estimated? Have we not at the South as well as the North, grown great, prosperous and happy under its operation? Has any part of the world ever shown such rapid progress in the development of wealth, and all the material resources of national power and greatness, as the southern States have under the general government, notwithstanding all its defects?

. . .

When I look around and see our prosperity in everything—agriculture, commerce, art, science, and every department of progress, physical, mental, and moral—certainly, in the face of such an exhibition, if we can, without the loss of power, or any essential right or interest, remain in the Union, it is our duty to ourselves and to posterity to do so. Let us not unwisely yield to this temptation. Our first parents, the great progenitors of the human race, were not without a like temptation when in the garden of Eden. They were led to believe that their condition would be bettered—that their eyes would be opened—and that they would become as gods. They in an evil hour yielded—instead of becoming gods, they only saw their own nakedness.

I look upon this country with our institutions as the Eden of the world, the Paradise of the universe. It may be that out of it, we may become greater and more prosperous, but I am candid and sincere in telling you that I fear if we yield to passion, and without sufficient cause, shall take that step, that instead of becoming greater or more peaceful, prosperous, and happy—instead of becoming gods, we will become demons, and at no distant day commence cutting one another's throats. This is my apprehension. Let us, therefore, whatever we do, meet these difficulties, great as they are, like wise and sensible men, and consider them in the light of all the consequences which may attend our action. Let us see first, clearly, where the path of duty leads, and then we may not fear to tread therein.

I come now to the main question put to me, and on which my counsel has been asked. That is, what the present legislature should do in view of the dangers that threaten us, and the wrongs that have been done us by several of our confederate States in the Union, by the acts of their legislatures nullifying the fugitive slave law, and in direct disregard of their constitutional obligations? What I shall say will not be in the spirit of dictation. It will be simply my own judgment for what it is worth. It proceeds from a strong conviction that according to it, our rights, interest, and honor—our present safety and future security can be maintained without yet looking to the last resort, the *"ultima ratio regum."* That should not be looked to until all else fails. That may come. On this point I am hopeful, but not sanguine. But let us use every patriotic effort to prevent it while there is ground for hope.

If any view that I may present, in your judgment, be inconsistent with the best interest of Georgia, I ask you as patriots not to regard it. After hearing me and others whom you have advised with, act in the premises according to your own conviction of duty as patriots. I speak now particularly to the members of the legislature present. There are, as I have said, great dangers ahead. Great dangers may come from the election I have spoken of. If the policy of Mr. Lincoln and his republican associates shall be carried out, or attempted to be carried out, no man in Georgia will be more willing or ready than myself to defend our rights, interest, and honor, at every hazard and to the last extremity. What is this policy? It is, in the first place, to exclude us, by an act of Congress, from the territories with our slave property. He is for using the power of the general government against the extension of our institutions. Our position on this point is, and ought to be, at all hazards, for perfect equality between all the States and the citizens of all the States in the territories, under the constitution of the

United States. If Congress should exercise its power against this, then I am for standing where Georgia planted herself in 1850. These were plain propositions which were then laid down in her celebrated platform, as sufficient for the disruption of the Union if the occasion should ever come; on these Georgia has declared that she will go out of the Union; and for these she would be justified by the nations of the earth in so doing. I say the same; I said it then; I say it now, if Mr. Lincoln's policy should be carried out. I have told you that I do not think his bare election sufficient cause; but if his policy should be carried out, in violation of any of the principles set forth in the Georgia platform, that would be such an act of aggression, which ought to be met as therein provided for. If his policy shall be carried out in repealing or modifying the fugitive slave law so as to weaken its efficacy, Georgia has declared that she will, in the last resort, disrupt the ties of the Union—and I say so too. I stand upon the Georgia platform, and upon every plank in it; and if these aggressions therein provided for take place, I say to you and to the people of Georgia, be ready for the assault when it comes; keep your powder dry, and let your assailants then have lead, if need be. I would wait for an act of aggression. This is my position.

. . .

Should Georgia determine to go out of the Union, I speak for one, though my views might not agree with them, whatever the result may be, I shall bow to the will of her people. Their cause is my cause, and their destiny is *my* destiny; and I trust this will be the ultimate course of all. The greatest curse that can befall a free people, is civil war.

But, as I said, let us call a convention of the people. Let all these matters be submitted to it, and when the will of a majority of the people has thus been expressed, the whole State will present one unanimous voice in favor of whatever may be demanded;

. . .

My position, then, in conclusion, is for the maintenance of the honor, the rights, the equality, the security, and the glory of my native State in the Union if possible; but if these cannot be maintained in the Union, then I am for their maintenance, at all hazards, out of it. Next to the honor and glory of Georgia, the land of my birth, I hold the honor and glory of our common country. In Savannah I was made to say by the reporters, who very often make me say things which I never did, that I was first for the glory of the whole country and next for that of Georgia. I said the exact reverse of this. I am proud of her history, of her present standing. I am proud even of her motto, which I would have duly respected at the present time by all her sons,—"Wisdom, Justice, and Moderation." I would have her rights and those of the Southern States maintained now upon these principles. Her position now is just what it was in 1850, with respect to the Southern States. Now I would add but one additional plank to that platform, which I have stated, and one which time has shown to be necessary; and if that shall likewise be adopted in substance by all the Southern States, all may yet be well. But if all this fails, we shall at least have the satisfaction of knowing that we have done our duty and all that patriotism could require.

. . .

DRAWING CONCLUSIONS:

1. What reasons are Stephens's argument for Georgia remaining in the Union? What does he warn will happen if Georgia does not secede?

2. What points does Stephens concede to the secessionists? On what points does he agree with secessionists like Cobb?

3. Review the points upon which Cobb and Stephens agree and disagree. How would you summarize the *key* disagreement between the two? What is Cobb's central argument for secession? What is Stephens's response? What is Stephens's central argument *for* the Union?

5.4 JOSEPH BROWN'S SECESSIONIST PUBLIC LETTER, DECEMBER 7, 1860

Governor Joseph E. Brown was born into humble circumstances and came of age in North Georgia, a hilly and mountainous region populated mainly by small landowning farm families with relatively few slave owners. As an ambitious young man, he worked his way through some of the most elite schools in the country until he finally earned a degree from the Yale School of Law. Brown rose through Georgia's political ranks by championing the small farmers of the North Georgia hills; and in 1857, he was elected the state's governor. By the time of the Civil War, Brown had achieved a degree of wealth and prosperity and had entered the ranks of the slaveholding class, but he remained something of an outsider among Georgia's slaveholding political elite. In late 1860, Brown came out in favor of Georgia's secession from the Union. In December, he issued a widely distributed public letter designed to persuade the non-slaveholders of North Georgia that they should support pro-secession candidates in the upcoming election for delegates to the January secession convention. Brown's letter offers an interesting example of how secession was sold to Georgia's non-slaveholding majority.

GUIDING QUESTIONS:

1. What is Brown's argument to non-slaveholders for Georgia's secession from the Union? What does he warn will happen if Georgia does not secede?
2. How does Brown's pro-secession argument (aimed at non-slaveholders) differ from Cobb's pro-secession argument (aimed at state legislators)?

*G*entlemen: Your letter requesting me to give to the people of Georgia my views upon the issues involved in the election of delegates to the State Convention, which is to assemble in January next, has been received.

Such is the extent of my official labors at present, that I can devote but little time to the preparation of a reply. If, however, any importance is attached to my opinions, in the present perilous times, I cheerfully give them to my fellow citizens. I propose to discuss briefly three propositions.

1st. Is the election of Mr. Lincoln to the Presidency, sufficient cause to justify Georgia and the other Southern States in seceding from the Union?

2d. What will be the results to the institution of slavery which will follow submission to the inauguration and administration of Mr. Lincoln as the President of one section of the Union?

3d. What will be the effect which the abolition of Slavery will have upon the interests and the social position of the large class of nonslaveholders and poor white laborers, who are in the South?

First, is the election of Mr. Lincoln sufficient cause to justify the secession of the Southern States from the Union? In my opinion the election of Mr. Lincoln, viewed only in the light of the triumph of a successful candidate, is not sufficient cause for a dissolution of the Union. This, however, is a very contracted and

William W. Freehling and Craig M. Simpson, eds., *Secession Debated: Georgia's Showdown in 1860* (New York: Oxford University Press, 1992), 147–159.

narrow view of the question. Mr. Lincoln is a mere mote in the great political atmosphere of the country, which, as it floats, only shows the direction in which the wind blows. He is the mere representative of a fanatical abolition sentiment—the mere instrument of a great triumphant political party, the principles of which are deadly hostile to the institution of Slavery, and openly at war with the fundamental doctrines of the Constitution of the United States. The rights of the South, and the institution of slavery, are not endangered by the triumph of Mr. Lincoln, the man; but they are in imminent danger from the triumph of the powerful party which he represents, and of the fanatical abolition sentiment which brought him into power, as the candidate of the Northern section of the Union, over the united opposition of the Southern section against him. The party embracing that sentiment, has constantly denied, and still denies, our equality in the Union, and our right to hold our slaves as property; and avows its purpose to take from us our property, so soon as it has the power. Its ability to elect Mr. Lincoln as its candidate, shows it now has the power to control the Executive branch of the Government. As the President, with the advice and consent of the Senate, appoints the Judges of the Supreme Court of the United States, when vacancies occur, its control of the Executive power will, in a few years, give it the control of the Judicial Department; while the constant increase of abolition sentiment, in the Northern States, now largely in the majority in Congress, together with the admission of other free States, will very soon, give it the power in the Legislative Department. The whole Government will then be in the hands of our enemies. The election of Mr. Lincoln is the first great step in this programme. It is the triumph of the Northern over the Southern section of the Union: of Northern fanaticism over Southern equality and Southern rights. While, therefore, the election of Mr. Lincoln, as a man, is no sufficient cause to justify secession, the triumph of the Northern section of the Union over the Southern section, upon a platform of avowed hostility to our rights, does, in my opinion, afford ample cause to justify the South in withdrawing from a confederacy where her equality, her honor, and the rights of her people, can no longer be protected.

Second, What will be the result to the institution of slavery, which will follow submission to the inauguration and administration of Mr. Lincoln as the President of one section of the Union? My candid opinion is, that it will be the total abolition of slavery, and the utter ruin of the South, in less than twenty-five years. If we submit now, we satisfy the Northern people that, come what may, we will never resist. If Mr. Lincoln places among us his Judges, District Attorneys, Marshals, Post Masters, Custom House officers, etc., etc., by the end of his administration, with the control of these men, and the distribution of public patronage, he will have succeeded in dividing us to an extent that will destroy all our moral powers, and prepare us to tolerate the running of a Republican ticket, in most of the States of the South, in 1864. If this ticket only secured five or ten thousand votes in each of the Southern States, it would be as large as the abolition party was in the North a few years since. It would hold a ballance [sic] of power between any two political parties into which the people of the South may hereafter be divided. This would soon give it the control of our elections. We would then be powerless, and the abolitionists would press forward, with a steady step, to the accomplishment of their object. They would refuse to admit any other slave States to the Union. They would abolish slavery in the District of Columbia, and at the Forts, Arsenals and Dock Yards, within the Southern States, which belong to the United States. They would then abolish the internal slave trade between the States, and prohibit a slave owner in Georgia from carrying his slaves into Alabama or South Carolina, and there selling them. These steps would be taken one at a time, cautiously, and our people would submit. Finally, when we were sufficiently humiliated, and sufficiently in their power, they would abolish slavery in the States. It will not be many years before enough of free States may be formed of the present territories of the United States, and admitted into the Union, to give them sufficient strength to change the Constitution, and remove all Constitutional barriers which now deny to Congress this power. I do not doubt, therefore, that submission to the administration of Mr. Lincoln will result in the final abolition of slavery. If we fail to resist now, we will never again have the strength to resist.

3rd, What effect will the abolition of slavery have upon the interest and social position of the large class of nonslaveholders and poor white laborers in the South? Here would be the scene of the most misery and ruin. Probably no one is so unjust as to say that it would be right to take from the slaveholder his property without paying for it. What would it cost to do this? There are, in round numbers, 4,500,000 slaves in the Southern States. They are worth, at a low estimate, 500 dollars each. All will agree to this. Multiply the 4,500,000 by the 500 and you have twenty-two hundred and fifty millions of dollars, which these slaves are worth. No one would agree that it is right to rob the Southern slaveholders of this vast sum of money without compensation. The Northern States would not agree to pay their proportion of the money, and the people of the South must be taxed to raise the money. If Georgia were only an average Southern State, she would have to pay one fifteenth part of this sum, which would be $150,000,000. Georgia is much more than an average State, and she must therefore pay a larger sum. Her people now pay less than half a million dollars a year, of tax. Suppose we had ten years within which to raise the $150,000,000, we would then have to raise, in addition to our present tax, $15,000,000 per annum, or over thirty times as much as we now pay.—The poor man, who now pays one dollar, would then have to pay $30.00. But suppose the Northern States agreed to help pay for these slaves, (who believes they would do it?) the share of Georgia would then be about one thirtieth of the twenty-two hundred and fifty millions of dollars, or over seventy-five millions; which, if raised in ten years, would be over fifteen times as much as our present tax. In this calculation, I have counted the slaveholder as taxed upon his own slaves to raise money to pay him for them. This would be a great injustice to him. If the sum is to be raised by the tax upon others, the nonslaveholders and poor white men of the South, would have to pay nearly the whole of this enormous sum, out of their labor. This would load them and their children with grievous indebtedness and heavy taxes for a long time to come. But suppose we were rid of this difficulty, what shall be done with these 4,500,000 negroes, when set free? Some of the Northern States have already passed laws prohibiting

free negroes from coming into their limits. They will help to harbor our runaway slaves, but will not receive among them our free negroes. They would not permit them to go there and live with them. Then what? One may say, send them to Africa. To such a proposition I might reply, send them to the moon. You may say that is not practicable. It is quite as much so as it is for us to pay for and send this vast number of negroes to Africa, with the means at our command.

No one would be so inhuman as to propose to send them to Africa and set them down upon a wild, naked sea coast, without provisions for at least one year. What will it cost to take them from their present home to Africa, and carry provisions there to keep them a single year? (if left with only one year's supply, many of them would starve to death.) It cannot be done for $250.00 each. At that sum it would amount to eleven hundred and twenty-five millions of dollars. Where will we get the money? Our people must be taxed to raise it. This would be half as large a sum as the above estimate to the value of the negroes. If the Southern States had it to raise Georgia's part would be over $75,000,000, which added to the part of the amount to be paid to owners for the negroes, would amount to $225,000,000; which must be raised by taxing the people, or loading them with a debt which would virtually enslave our whole people for generations to come. It must be remembered that we own no territory in Africa large enough to colonize 4,500,000 people. This too must be bought at a very heavy cost. The Northern people would not consent to be taxed to raise these enormous sums, either to pay for the negroes, or to pay for sending them to Africa, or to pay for land upon which to colonize them; as they do not wish to do either. They wish to take them from their owners without pay, and set them free, and let them remain among us. Many people at the North, say that negroes are our fit associates; that they shall be set free, and remain among us—intermarrying with our children, and enjoying equal privileges with us. But suppose we were over the difficulty of paying the owners for the negroes, and they were taken from their masters without pay, and set free and left among us, (which is the ultimate aim of the Black Republicans,) what would be the effect upon our society? We should still have rich men and poor men. But few of slave owners have invested all they have in negroes. Take their negroes from them unjustly, and they will many of them still be more wealthy than their neighbors. If all were left for a time with equal wealth, every person who has noticed man and society knows that, in a few years, some would grow rich and others poor. This has always been the case, and always will be. If we had no negroes, the rich would still be in a better condition to take care of themselves than the poor. They would still seek the most profitable and secure investment for their capital. What would this be? The answer suggests itself to every mind: it would be land. The wealthy would soon buy all the lands of the South worth cultivating. Then what? The poor would all become tenants, as they are in England, the New England States, and all old countries where slavery does not exist. But I must not lose sight of the 4,500,000 free negroes to be turned loose among us. They, too, must become tenants, with the poor white people for they would not be able to own lands. A large proportion of them would spend their time in idleness and vice, and would live by stealing, robbing and plundering. Probably one fourth of the whole number would have to be maintained in our penitentiary, prisons, and poor houses. Our people, poor and rich, must be taxed to pay the expenses of imprisoning and punishing them for crime. They would have to begin the world miserable poor, with neither land, money nor provisions. They must therefore become day laborers for their old masters, or such others as would employ them. In this capacity they would at once come in competition with the poor white laborers. Men of capital would see this, and fix the price of labor accordingly. The negro has only been accustomed to receive his victuals and clothes for his labor. Few of them, if free, would expect anything more. If would therefore be easy to employ them at a sum sufficient to supply only the actual necessaries of life. The poor white man would then go to the wealthy land-owner and say, I wish employment. Hire me to work. I have a wife and children who must have bread. The land-owner would offer probably twenty cents per day. The laborer would say, I cannot support my family on that sum. The landlord replies, That is not my business. I am sorry for you, but I must look to my own interest. The black man who lives on my land has as strong an arm, and as heavy muscles as you have, and can do as much labor. He works for me at that rate, you must work for the same price, or I cannot employ you. The negro comes into competition with the white man and fixes the price of his labor, and he must take it or get no employment.

Again, the poor white man wishes to rent land from the wealthy landlord—this landlord asks him half the crop of common upland or two thirds or even three fourths, for the best bottom land. The poor man says this seems very hard. I cannot make a decent support for my family at these rates. The landlord replies, here are negroes all around me anxious to take it at these rates; I can let you have it for no less. The negro therefore, comes into competition with the poor white man, when he seeks to rent land on which to make his bread, or a shelter to protect his wife and his little ones, from the cold and from the rain; and when he seeks employment as a day laborer. In every such case if the negro will do the work the cheapest, he must be preferred. It is sickening to contemplate the miseries of our poor white people under these circumstances. They now get higher wages for their labor than the poor of any other country on the globe. Most of them are land owners, and they are now respected. They are in no sense placed down upon a level with the negro. They are a superior race, and they feel and know it. Abolish slavery, and you make the negroes their equals, legally and socially (not naturally, for no human law can change God's law) and you very soon make them all tenants, and reduce their wages for daily labor to the smallest pittance that will sustain life. Then the negro and the white man, and their families, must labor in the field together as equals. Their children must go to the same poor school together, if they are educated at all. They must go to church as equals; enter the Courts of justice as equals, sue and be sued as equals, sit on juries together as equals, have the right to give evidence in Court as equals, stand side by side in our military corps as equals, enter each others' houses in social intercourse as equals; and very soon their children must marry together as equals. May our kind Heavenly Father avert the evil, and deliver the poor from such a fate. So soon as the slaves were at liberty, thousands of them would leave the cotton and rice fields in the lower parts of our State, and make their way to the healthier climate in the mountain region. We should have them plundering and stealing, robbing and killing, in all the lovely vallies of the mountains. This I can never consent to see. The mountains contain the place of my nativity, the home of my manhood, and the theatre of most of the acts of my life; and I can never forget the condition and interest of the people who reside there. It is true, the people there are generally poor; but they are brave, honest, patriotic, and pure hearted. Some who do not know them, have doubted their capacity to understand these questions, and their patriotism and valor to defend their rights when invaded. I know them well, and I know that no greater mistake could be made. They love the Union of our fathers, and would never consent to dissolve it so long as the constitution is not violated, and so long as it protects their rights; but they love liberty and justice more; and they will never consent to submit to abolition rule, and permit the evils to come upon them, which must result from a continuance in the Union when the government is in the hands of our enemies, who will use all its power for our destruction. When it becomes necessary to defend our rights against so foul a domination, I would call upon the mountain boys as well as the people of the lowlands, and they would come down like an avalanche and swarm around the flag of Georgia with a resolution that would strike terror into the ranks of the abolition cohorts of the North. Wealth is timid, and wealthy men may cry for peace, and submit to wrong for fear they may lose their money: but the poor, honest laborers of Georgia, can never consent to see slavery abolished, and submit to all the taxation, vassalage, low wages and downright degradation, which must follow. They will never take the negro's place; God forbid.

I know that some contemptible demagogues have attempted to deceive them by appealing to their prejudices, and asking them what interest they have in maintaining the rights of the wealthy slaveholder. They cannot be deceived in this way. They know that the government of our State protects their lives, their families and their property; and that every dollar the wealthy slaveholder has, may be taken by the government of the State, if need be, to protect the rights and liberties of all. One man, in a large neighborhood, has a mill. Not one in fifty has a mill. What would be thought of the public speaker who would appeal to the fifty, and ask them what interest they have in defending their neighbor's mill, if an abolition mob were trying to burn it down? Another has a store. Not one in fifty has a store. Who would say the fifty should not help the one if an invader is about to burn his store? Another has a blacksmith shop. Not one in fifty has a blacksmith shop. Shall the shop be destroyed by the common enemy and no one protect the owner because no one near, has the same peculiar kind of property? It may be that I have no horse, and you have a horse; or that I have a cow, and you have no cow. In such case, if our rights of property are assailed by a common enemy, shall we not help each other? Or I have a wife and children, and a house, and another has neither wife and children, nor house. Will he, therefore, stand by and see my house burned and my wife and children butchered, because he has none? The slaveholder has honestly invested the money, which it has cost him years of toil to make, in slaves, which are guaranteed to him by the laws of our State. The common enemy of the South seeks to take the property from him. Shall all who do not own slaves, stand by and permit it to be done? If so, they have no right to call on the slaveholder, by taxation, or otherwise, to help protect their property or their liberties. Such a doctrine is monstrous; and he who would advocate it, deserves to be rode upon the sharpest edge of one of Lincoln's rails. The doctrine strikes at the very foundation of society, and if carried out, would destroy all property, and all protection to life, liberty and happiness.

The present is a critical time with the people of the South. We all, rich and poor, have a common interest, a common destiny. It is no time to be wrangling about old party strifes. Our common enemy, the Black Republican party, is united and triumphant. Let us all unite. If we cannot all see alike, let us have charity enough towards each other, to admit that all are equally patriotic in their efforts to advance the common cause. My honest convictions are, that we can never again live in peace with the Northern abolitionists, unless we can have new constitutional guarantees, which will secure our equal rights in the Territories, and effectually stop the discussion of the slavery question in Congress, and secure the rendition of fugitive slaves. These guarantees I do not believe the people of the Northern States will ever give, while we remain together in the Union. Their opinion is, that we will always compromise away a portion of our rights, and submit, for the sake of peace. If the Cotton States would all secede from the Union before the inauguration of Mr. Lincoln, this might possibly lead to a Convention of all the States, which might terminate in a reunion with the new constitutional guarantees necessary for our protection. If the Northern States then failed to give these guarantees, there can be no doubt that Virginia, Maryland, North Carolina, Delaware, Kentucky, Missouri, and Tennessee would unite with the Cotton States in a Southern Confederacy and we should form a Republic in which, under the old Constitution of our fathers, our people could live in security and peace. I know that many of our people honestly believe that it would be best to wait for these border slave States to go out with us. If we wait for this, we shall *submit*; for some of those States will not consent to go, and the North will then consent to give us no new guarantees of peace. They will say that we have again blustered and submitted, as we always do.

In my late message to the General Assembly, I recommended the enactment of retalitory [sic] laws against these Northern States which have nullified the fugitive slave law. I think those laws should still be enacted. They would have been equally applicable had either of the other candidates for the Presidency been successful. Now that Mr. Lincoln is successful, they should be upon our staute [*sic*] book, so long as we remain in the Union. There can no longer be a reasonable doubt, that the gallant State of South Carolina will secede from the Union very soon after her Convention meets. The States of Florida, Alabama and Mississippi will follow in quick succession. While our Convention is in session, we shall probably be surrounded on every side but one, with free and independent States out of the Union. With these States, we have a common interest. Thus surrounded, shall Georgia remain under abolition rule, and refuse to unite with her sister States around her? I trust not. If so, we forfeit all claim to our proud title of Empire State of the South. Why remain? Will the Northern States repeal their personal liberty bills and do us justice? No. The Legislature of one of the nullifing

[*sic*] States (Vermont) has just adjourned. A bill has been introduced for the repeal of those unconstitutional and offensive laws. The question has been discussed, and it is reported that the House in which the bill was introduced, has refused to pass the repealing law, by a vote of over two-thirds. This action has been had with full knowledge of the state of things now existing in the South, and shows a deliberate determination not to do us justice. Is further notice to Vermont necessary? I am aware that the fears of some have been appealed to, and they have been told that if we secede, the United States Government will attempt to coerce us back into the Union, and we shall have war.

The President in his late message, while he denies our Constitutional right to secede, admits that the General Government has no Constitutional right to coerce us back into the Union, if we do secede. Secession is not likely, therefore, to involve us in war. Submission may. When the other States around us secede, if we remain in the Union, thousands of our people will leave the State, and it is feared that the standard of revolution and rebellion may be raised among us, which would at once involve us in civil war among ourselves. If we must fight, in the name of all that is sacred, let us fight our common enemy, and not fight each other.

In my opinion, our people should send their wisest and best men to the Convention, without regard to party distinctions, and should intrust much to their good judgment and sound discretion, when they meet. They may, then, have new lights before them, which we do not now have; and they should be left free to act upon them.

My fervent prayer is, that the God of our fathers may inspire the Convention with wisdom, and so direct their counsels as to protect our rights and preserve our liberties to the latest generation.

I am, gentlemen, with great respect,

Your fellow citizen,

Joseph E. Brown

DRAWING CONCLUSION:

1. How does Brown's pro-secession argument differ from Cobb's? What does this reveal about how secession was sold to non-slaveowners?

5.5   ALEXANDER STEPHENS, EXCERPTS FROM "THE CORNERSTONE SPEECH," MARCH 21, 1861

Alexander Stephens served as a delegate to Georgia's January 1861 secession convention where he argued and voted against the state's secession from the Union. Following Georgia's declaration of independence, however, Stephens proclaimed his loyalty to the state and was elected as one of Georgia's representatives to the founding Congress of the Confederate State of America, which convened in early February 1861. Later that month, the Congress elected Stephens to the office of Confederate Vice President. In March, Stephens returned to Georgia; and on the 21st of that month, he delivered a public address in the city of Savannah, an address that came to be known at the "Cornerstone Speech." By the time of this speech, the prospect of war over the issue of Confederate independence was becoming increasingly likely. The speech can thus be thought of as an effort to rally the public for the struggles that lay ahead. To accomplish this goal, Stephens focused his address on the ways that the new Confederate Constitution, in his view, was superior to the old United States Constitution. He points to one particular characteristic of the Confederate Constitution as the greatest and most important improvement over the old US Constitution. In fact, he refers to this characteristic of the Confederate Constitution as the "cornerstone" of the Confederacy.

GUIDING QUESTIONS:

1. What does Stephens argue is the most important way in which the new Confederate Constitution was an improvement over the old United States Constitution?
2. What does Stephens declare to be the "cornerstone" of the Confederacy?

EXCERPTS FROM THE "CORNERSTONE SPEECH"

Alexander Stephens

SPEECH DELIVERED ON THE 21ST OF MARCH, 1861, IN SAVANNAH, KNOWN AS "THE CORNER STONE SPEECH," REPORTED IN THE *SAVANNAH REPUBLICAN*.

At half past seven o'clock on Thursday evening, the largest audience ever assembled at the Athenaeum was in the house, waiting most impatiently for the appearance of the orator of the evening, Honorable A. H. Stephens, Vice-President of the Confederate States of America. The committee, with invited guests, were seated on the stage, when, at the appointed hour, the Honorable C. C. Jones, Mayor, and the speaker, entered, and were greeted by the immense assemblage with deafening rounds of applause.

The Mayor then, in a few pertinent remarks, introduced Mr. Stephens, stating that at the request of a number of the members of the convention, and citizens of Savannah and the State, now here, he had consented to address them upon the present state of public affairs.

Mr. Stephens rose and said:

Mr. Mayor, and Gentlemen of the Committee, and Fellow-Citizens: For this reception you will please

From Henry Cleveland, *Alexander H. Stephens in Public and Private* (Philadelphia: National Publishing Company, 1866), 71–718, 721–723.

accept my most profound and sincere thanks. The compliment is doubtless intended as such, or more, perhaps, in honor of the occasion, and my public position, in connection with the great events now crowding upon us, than to me personally and individually. It is however none the less appreciated by me on that account. We are in the midst of one of the greatest epochs in our history. The last ninety days will mark one of the most memorable eras in the history of modern civilization.

. . .

I was remarking, that we are passing through one of the greatest revolutions in the annals of the world. Seven States have within the last three months thrown off an old government and formed a new. This revolution has been signally marked, up to this time, by the fact of its having been accomplished without the loss of a single drop of blood. [Applause.]

This new constitution, or form of government, constitutes the subject to which your attention will be partly invited. In reference to it, I make this first general remark. It amply secures all our ancient rights, franchises, and liberties. All the great principles of Magna Charta are retained in it. No citizen is deprived of life, liberty, or property, but by the judgment of his peers under the laws of the land. The great principle of religious liberty, which was the honor and pride of the old constitution, is still maintained and secured. All the essentials of the old constitution, which have endeared it to the hearts of the American people, have been preserved and perpetuated. [Applause.] Some changes have been made. Of these I shall speak presently. Some of these I should have preferred not to have seen made; but these, perhaps, meet the cordial approbation of a majority of this audience, if not an overwhelming majority of the people of the Confederacy. Of them, therefore, I will not speak. But other important changes do meet my cordial approbation. They form great improvements upon the old constitution. So, taking the whole new constitution, I have no hesitancy in giving it as my judgment that it is decidedly better than the old. [Applause.]

. . .

But not to be tedious in enumerating the numerous changes for the better, allow me to allude to one other—though last, not least. The new constitution has put at rest, forever, all the agitating questions relating to our peculiar institution—African slavery as it exists amongst us—the proper *status* of the negro in our form of civilization. This was the immediate cause of the late rupture and present revolution. Jefferson in his forecast, had anticipated this, as the "rock upon which the old Union would split." He was right. What was conjecture with him, is now a realized fact. But whether he fully comprehended the great truth upon which that rock *stood* and *stands*, may be doubted. The prevailing ideas entertained by him and most of the leading statesmen at the time of the formation of the old constitution, were that the enslavement of the African was in violation of the laws of nature; that it was wrong in *principle*, socially, morally, and politically. It was an evil they knew not well how to deal with, but the general opinion of the men of that day was that, somehow or other in the order of Providence, the institution would be evanescent and pass away. This idea, though not incorporated in the constitution, was the prevailing idea at that time. The constitution, it is true, secured every essential guarantee to the institution while it should last, and hence no argument can be justly urged against the constitutional guarantees thus secured, because of the common sentiment of the day. Those ideas, however, were fundamentally wrong. They rested upon the assumption of the equality of races. This was an error. It was a sandy foundation, and the government built upon it fell when the "storm came and the wind blew."

Our new government is founded upon exactly the opposite idea; its foundations are laid, its cornerstone rests upon the great truth, that the negro is not equal to the white man; that slavery—subordination to the superior race—is his natural and normal condition. [Applause.]

This, our new government, is the first, in the history of the world, based upon this great physical, philosophical, and moral truth. This truth has been slow in the process of its development, like all other truths in the various departments of science. It has been so even amongst us. Many who hear me, perhaps, can recollect well, that this truth was not generally admitted, even within their day. The errors of the past generation still clung to many as late as twenty years ago. Those at the North, who still cling to these errors, with a zeal above knowledge, we justly denominate fanatics. All fanaticism springs from an aberration of the mind—from a defect in reasoning. It is a species of insanity. One of the most striking characteristics of insanity, in many instances, is forming correct conclusions from fancied or erroneous premises; so with the anti-slavery fanatics; their conclusions are right if their premises were. They assume that the negro is equal, and hence conclude that he is entitled to equal privileges and rights with the white man. If their premises were correct, their conclusions would be logical and just—but their premise being wrong, their whole argument fails. I recollect once of having heard a gentleman from one of the northern States, of great power and ability, announce in the House of Representatives, with imposing effect, that we of the South would be compelled, ultimately, to yield upon this subject of slavery, that it was as impossible to war successfully against a principle in politics, as it was in physics or mechanics. That the principle would ultimately prevail. That we, in maintaining slavery as it exists with us, were warring against a principle, a principle founded in nature, the principle of the equality of men. The reply I made to him was, that upon his own grounds, we should, ultimately, succeed, and that he and his associates, in this crusade against our institutions, would ultimately fail. The truth announced, that it was as impossible to war successfully against a principle in politics as it was in physics and mechanics, I admitted; but told him that it was he, and those acting with him, who were warring against a principle. They were attempting to make things equal which the Creator had made unequal.

In the conflict thus far, success has been on our side, complete throughout the length and breadth of the Confederate States. It is upon this, as I have stated, our social fabric is firmly planted; and I cannot permit myself to doubt the ultimate success of a full recognition of this principle throughout the civilized and enlightened world.

As I have stated, the truth of this principle may be slow in development, as all truths are and ever have been, in the various branches of science. It was

so with the principles announced by Galileo—it was so with Adam Smith and his principles of political economy. It was so with Harvey, and his theory of the circulation of the blood. It is stated that not a single one of the medical profession, living at the time of the announcement of the truths made by him, admitted them. Now, they are universally acknowledged. May we not, therefore, look with confidence to the ultimate universal acknowledgment of the truths upon which our system rests? It is the first government ever instituted upon the principles in strict conformity to nature, and the ordination of Providence, in furnishing the materials of human society. Many governments have been founded upon the principle of the subordination and serfdom of certain classes of the same race; such were and are in violation of the laws of nature. Our system commits no such violation of nature's laws. With us, all of the white race, however high or low, rich or poor, are equal in the eye of the law. Not so with the negro. Subordination is his place. He, by nature, or by the curse against Canaan, is fitted for that condition which he occupies in our system. The architect in the construction of buildings, lays the foundation with the proper material—the granite; then comes the brick or the marble. The substratum of our society is made of the material fitted by nature for it, and by experience we know, that it is best, not only for the superior, but for the inferior race, that it should be so. It is, indeed, in conformity with the ordinance of the Creator. It is not for us to inquire into the wisdom of his ordinances, or to question them. For his own purposes, he has made one race to differ from another, as he has made "one star to differ from another star in glory."

The great objects of humanity are best attained when there is conformity to his laws and decrees, in the formation of governments as well as in all things else. Our confederacy is founded upon principles in strict conformity with these laws. This stone which was rejected by the first builders "is become the chief of the corner"—the real "corner-stone"—in our new edifice. [Applause.]

I have been asked, what of the future? It has been apprehended by some that we would have arrayed against us the civilized world. I care not who or how many they may be against us, when we stand upon the eternal principles of truth, if we are true to ourselves and the principles for which we contend, we are obliged to, and must triumph. [Immense applause.]

Thousands of people who begin to understand these truths are not yet completely out of the shell; they do not see them in their length and breadth. We hear much of the civilization and christianization of the barbarous tribes of Africa. In my judgment, those ends will never be attained, but by first teaching them the lesson taught to Adam, that "in the sweat of his brow he should eat his bread," [applause] and teaching them to work, and feed, and clothe themselves.

DRAWING CONCLUSION:

1. What does Stephens's "Cornerstone Speech" reveal about the motives of secessionists in the state of Georgia?

LINCOLN'S OPTIONS

Lincoln was elected president on November 6, 1860. By the time he took office the following March, seven southern states had seceded and formed the Confederate States of America. Between November and March, Lincoln and his fellow Republicans had to determine how to respond to the growing secessionist tide in the South. And upon taking office on March 4, 1861, he had to decide how to respond to the fact of secession. Lincoln and the Republicans had a number of options. They could, for instance, have simply accepted secession and recognized Confederate independence. Lincoln, however, rejected this option on the grounds that secession was an act of rebellion with no legal or constitutional basis. Lincoln could have sought a political compromise that might have persuaded southern political leaders to abandon secession. Lincoln was willing to seek compromise on certain items. On the key issue of the expansion of slavery into the territories of the West, though, he declared himself inflexible. In the end, following the Confederate assault on Fort Sumter, Lincoln employed force to suppress the rebellion. Determining why Lincoln rejected both secession and compromise, and why in the end he responded with force, is central to determining the causes of the Civil War.

6.1 REPUBLICAN NEWSPAPER EDITORIALS

Republican responses to secession can be gauged through the editorials published in Republican newspapers during the secession crisis. As the newly elected Republican president, Lincoln's perspective on secession would be influenced by the views of those within his party.

GUIDING QUESTIONS:

1. How did the writers of these Republican newspaper editorials view the growing secessionist movement in the South? Look for common patterns.
2. How did the tone of the editorials change over time? Pay close attention to the dates of each editorial?

HARTFORD EVENING PRESS, OCTOBER 26, 1860

It seems almost absurd to lay down definite principles on the subject of disunion. Disunion is a threat, not an argument. When a man begins to threaten, he gives up the argument; he confesses that his reasons are worthless, and that he has no mode left of accomplishing his purpose except brute force. When, therefore, northern democrats tell us that disunion is to be the consequence of the election of a republican president, we need not suppose that they desire or recommend it, but merely that they are afraid that southern politicians will bring it to pass. How much, then, is it best to be frightened?

We say, not at all; the threat is an empty sham; those who make it have not the remotest intention of fulfilling it; or if a few of them have, their enterprise has about as good a chance of succeeding as the lunatics in the Retreat at Hartford would have of capsizing the state of Connecticut into Long Island Sound. They are too few and too crazy.

If the threat is worth regarding; if the purpose is earnest, the meaning of such a state of things is serious indeed. In that case, it means that the great political experiment of these United States is *a great failure;* that the will of a peaceful voting majority can no longer govern the nation; that any minority wicked enough and desperate enough can govern us on the great principle of a pirate in a powder magazine, who will blow the ship to atoms if his orders are not complied with. Now, of all the hateful despotisms in the world, none is so infernally hateful as an oligarchy; even Nero was not so bad as the thirty tyrants; and if an attempt is to be made to subject our thirty millions of people to the arbitrary will of three hundred thousand tyrants—for that is about the number of slave-holders—every independent, honest northern mind must desire that this issue be made NOW, *met promptly,* and decided once for all. We are ready for the decision. And we fully believe that when given, while it would result in the annihilation of the shallow traitorous fools, it would only consolidate more firmly the national power. These men say to us, acquiesce in one wickedness or we will commit another. If the Union has arrived at such a state of moral imbecility that its voters can be frightened into a course of action by such a choice of wickedness as this, it is high time that the fact were fully proved.

But, it may be urged, disunion is threatened in consequence of the unconstitutional measures proposed by the Republicans. We answer that we defy any man to point out any measure proposed by any Republican leader which is not constitutional.

From Howard Cecil Perkins, ed., *Northern Editorials on Secession*, vol. 1 (New York: D. Appleton-Century Company, 1942).

PITTSBURGH GAZETTE, NOVEMBER 14, 1860

THE DISUNION RANT

The true way to treat the Disunion bluster now so prevalent at the South, is to leave it alone. The attempt to resist it or put it down by force, would assist instead of repress it, and make that real which is now only a sham.

The Disunion cry has been the bugaboo of the South for thirty years. With it she has always, hitherto, been able to scare the North into submission; and the sole object of resorting to it in the late election was to drive the North into compliance with her wishes. The noisy blusterers of the South had no doubt of their ability to accomplish their end. Failure was never anticipated, not even dreamed of by them.

But they *have* failed. Had they succeeded, the hollowness of their threats would never have been discovered; but having failed, the sole question with them now is, how best to escape from their embarrassing position. They must do *something*, to make their people at home believe them in earnest, and yet so manage it as to prevent the consummation of what they threaten.

This is the explanation of the present attitude of the South. The leaders—Toombs, Yancey, Chesnut, Iverson, Wise and the other noisy fellows, who declared without reservation that the election of Lincoln would be followed by a dissolution of the Union, must either attempt to dissolve it or go into utter disgrace. They are therefore pretending to carry their threats into execution in order to put themselves right at home. They have promised; and they must at least *seem* to perform.

It would be the madness of folly, therefore, to treat these men as being in earnest. To do that would soon make them in earnest. Let them alone and play out their play. When they show signs of being in earnest, and put their necks in a halter, it will be time enough to string them up. They will not do that, if left to themselves. They have been, for years, engaged with the zeal of demagogues in inflaming the public mind of the South with artful misrepresentations of Northern sentiment and designs, and extravagant appeals to Southern peculiarities; and now, when the crisis has come which they have provoked, but not anticipated, they find themselves confronted by a people who have taken them at their word and have not only believed, but profess a willingness to follow, them. How shall the poor devils escape? That is a question for *them* to answer. Let us rather sympathize with them in their dilemma than think of dealing severely with them. They must wriggle out of their trouble; and it will be amusing to stand by and witness their manoeuvres in doing so.

In less than a month this farce will be played out. Within that time the true Union sentiment of the South will develop itself. There is patriotism and good sense enough in the South to manage the whole affair. Let us leave it, then, in the hands of the true men of the South. It does not need our interference. Hands off. The time *may* come when the whole country will have to interfere; but just now all that the North has to do is to leave the Hotspurs alone.

BUFFALO EVENING EXPRESS, JANUARY 5, 1861

The people of the Northern States are slow to anger. Their blood moves tardily, but we begin to see indications that it is warming up under the influence of Southern depredations upon the Constitution and the integrity of the Union. The course pursued by South Carolina against the flag of the United States, the seizing of the forts—the running up of piratical colors in place of the stars and stripes—the assuming of federal powers over the port by the rebels—the obstruction of the harbor—the erection of fortifications to be brought to bear upon the federal troops and forts—the imbecility of the President, and a sense of deep wrong to the Constitution and the Union, all conspire to awaken the people of the North to a sense of duty and danger. We have no hope left of any conciliatory measures which will avert the impending calamities. South Carolina has gone too far to recede. She rushes madly into the vortex of her own destruction. She defies the federal power—insults the federal flag—seizes the federal forts—turns their guns upon federal troops,—and is guilty of acts which are alike injurious and insulting to the United States. This the people of the North, who are devoted to the Constitution and the laws, and have lived for the Union in the midst of evil as well as good report, have borne, until forbearance has ceased to be a virtue. These insults to the flag of our country will not be brooked for any length of time. These defiant threats of haughty Southrons against Northern prowess, begin to take effect upon Northern blood. The North—the Northeast—and the Northwest have stood calmly and witnessed these assaults upon the integrity of the Nation, until the fires of '76 begin to be relighted in New England hearts, and the love of country and pride of nation excites men of the North and Northwest to stern determinations and a desire for action in rebuke and punishment of these overt acts of treason. Not one man in fifty now will stop to reflect upon a plan of compromise or pacification. Almost every man feels that his country and its institutions have been wronged—that treason is abroad, and that no alternative remains, but for men of courage and patriotism to meet force with force until this question shall be settled effectually, and in a manner that shall leave the bond of union in the States unbroken.

Men may talk and bluster of breaking up this Union, but it cannot be done. South Carolina may pass ordinances of secession, and assume a hostile attitude towards the federal government—her ragged battalions may erect fortifications, and the General QUATTLEBUMS of the South, covered with gold lace and feathers, may inveigh against the federal power, but all these things must be answered for to the people of the North who stand inflexibly by the Union. There is no escaping condign punishment in the end. The time will come when bluster will be of little avail and menaces will be laughed at. Then the mighty hosts of the far North will sweep over the region of Slavery with a power that cannot be resisted. We have the resources, physical and financial, to preserve this government, and under the blessings of a just God it will be preserved against treason and rebellion. When this blow is struck, and blood is shed, we can place the date of the beginning of the end of slavery on this continent. That institution can never survive a collision of States. It must fall as assuredly as that God is just. Its friends and defenders should know and consider this well, before they push the issue to extremity.

The present attitude of affairs in South Carolina has a warlike tendency at the North. No war has ever yet broken out on this continent in which Northern blood has not mingled, and when we find our troops menaced with danger from rebels, there is a strong feeling here which looks to their relief. In this connection we expect daily to see recruiting stations opened in our city, under the stripes and stars, for volunteers to defend the government against treason. The men are ready—and twenty days may find a regiment of one thousand men ready to march from this city southward in defence of the Constitution and the Union.

DRAWING CONCLUSION:

1. What do these newspaper editorials reveal about Republican response to secession?

6.2 HORACE GREELEY AND SECESSION

Horace Greeley of the *New York Tribune* was the country's most prominent and influential Republican newspaper editor. Three days after Lincoln's election, Greeley published an editorial in which he declared that if the cotton states desired to depart the Union that they should be allowed to "go in peace." This editorial could be taken as evidence that at least some Republicans were willing to see the Union dissolved. A closer reading of the editorial, however, reveals that Greeley set numerous conditions that he believed must be met before a peaceable dissolution of the Union could be entertained. Furthermore, by the following February, Greeley had dropped all talk of peaceable separation. An examination of Greeley's evolving stance on secession can provide important clues into the stance of northern Republicans.

The first document is Greeley's famous "Go in Peace" editorial, published just after the November election. The second is an account of an exchange between Greeley and Lincoln in December of 1860. (The account is taken from the memoirs of John G. Nicolay and John Hay, Lincoln's personal secretary and assistant secretary.) In the account, Greeley clarifies his stance with regard to secession. The final document is an editorial that Greeley published in February 1861 in which all talk of peaceable separation was gone. Pay close attention to Greeley's actual position on secession and how it evolved over time.

GUIDING QUESTIONS:

1. What conditions did Greeley set on "peaceable separation" in his "Go in Peace" editorial?
2. What did Horace Greeley tell Lincoln was the true motivation for his "go in peace" position?
3. By February and March of 1861, what was Greeley's position on secession and the proper federal response to it?

EDITORIAL IN *NEW YORK TRIBUNE*, NOVEMBER 9, 1860

"GOING TO GO.—The people of the United States have indicated, according to the forms prescribed by the Constitution, their desire that Abraham Lincoln, of Illinois, shill be their next President, and Hannibal Hamlin, of Maine, their Vice-President. A very large plurality of the popular vote has been cast for them, and a decided majority of Electors chosen, who will undoubtedly vote for and elect them on the first Wednesday in December next. The electoral votes will be formally sealed up and forwarded to Washington, there to be opened and counted, on a given day in February next, in the presence of both Houses of Congress; and it will then be the duty of Mr. John C. Breckinridge, as President of the Senate, to declare Lincoln and Hamlin duly elected President and Vice-President of these United States.

"Some people do not like this, as is very natural. Dogberry discovered, a good while ago, that "When two ride a horse, one must ride behind." That is not generally deemed the preferable seat; but the rule remains unaffected by that circumstance. We know how to sympathize with the defeated; for we remember how *we* felt, when Adams was defeated; and Clay, and Scott, and Frémont. It is decidedly pleasanter to be on the winning side, especially when—as now—it happens also to be the *right* side.

From *New York Tribune*, November 9, 1860.

"We sympathize with the afflicted; but we cannot recommend them to do any thing desperate. What is the use? They are beaten now; they may triumph next time: in fact, they have generally had their own way: had they been subjected to the discipline of adversity so often as we have, they would probably bear it with more philosophy, and deport themselves more befittingly. We live to learn: and one of the most difficult acquirements is that of meeting reverses with graceful fortitude.

"The telegraph informs us that most of the Cotton States are meditating a withdrawal from the Union, because of Lincoln's election. Very well: they have a right to meditate, and meditation is a profitable employment of leisure. We have a chronic, invincible disbelief in Disunion as a remedy for either Northern or Southern grievances. We cannot see any necessary connection between the alleged disease and this ultraheroic remedy; still, we say, if any one sees fit to meditate Disunion, let him do so unmolested. That was a base and hypocritic row that was once raised, at Southern dictation, about the ears of John Quincy Adams, because he presented a petition for the dissolution of the Union. The petitioner had a right to make the request; it was the Member's duty to present it. And now, if the Cotton States consider the value of the Union debatable, we maintain their perfect right to discuss it. Nay: we hold, with Jefferson, to the inalienable right of communities to alter or abolish forms of government that have become oppressive or injurious; and, if the Cotton States shall decide that they can do better out of the Union than in it, we insist on letting them go in peace. The right to secede may be a revolutionary one, but it exists nevertheless; and we do not see how one party can have a right to do what another party has a right to prevent. We must ever resist the asserted right of any State to remain in the Union, and nullify or defy the laws thereof: to withdraw from the Union is quite another matter. And, whenever a considerable section of our Union shall deliberately resolve to go out, we shall resist all coercive measures designed to keep it in. We hope never to live in a republic, whereof one section is pinned to the residue by bayonets.

"But, while we thus uphold the practical liberty, if not the abstract right, of secession, we must insist that the step be taken, if it ever shall be, with the deliberation and gravity befitting so momentous an issue. Let ample time be given for reflection; let the subject be fully canvassed before the people; and let a popular vote be taken in every case, before Secession is decreed. Let the people be told just why they are asked to break up the confederation; let them have both sides of the question fully presented; let them reflect, deliberate, then vote; and let the act of Secession be the echo of an unmistakable popular fiat. A judgment thus rendered, a demand for separation so backed, would either be acquiesced in without the effusion of blood, or those who rushed upon carnage to defy and defeat it, would place themselves clearly in the wrong.

"The measures now being inaugurated in the Cotton States, with a view (apparently) to Secession, seem to us destitute of gravity and legitimate force. They bear the unmistakable impress of haste—of passion—of distrust of the popular judgment. They seem clearly intended to precipitate the South into rebellion before the baselessness of the clamors which have misled and excited her, can be ascertained by the great body of her people. We trust that they will be confronted with calmness, with dignity, and with unwavering trust in the inherent strength of the Union, and the loyalty of the American people."

NICOLAY AND HAY RECOUNT LINCOLN AND GREELEY'S EXCHANGE ON SECESSION

Mr. Greeley was, as we have seen, indulging in damaging vagaries about peaceable secession, and to him Lincoln sent a word of friendly caution. Greeley wrote a statement of his views in reply, but substantially yielded the point. He said a State could no more secede at pleasure from the Union than a stave could secede from a cask. That if eight or ten contiguous States sought to leave, he should say, "There's the door — go!" But, "if the seceding State or States go to fighting and defying the laws, the Union being

---

From John G. Nicolay and John Hay, *Abraham Lincoln: A History*, vol. 3 (New York: The Century Company, 1904), 258.

yet undissolved save by their own say-so, I guess they will have to be made to behave themselves. . . . I fear nothing, care for nothing, but another disgraceful back-down of the free States. That is the only real danger. Let the Union slide — it may be reconstructed; let Presidents be assassinated, we can elect more; let the Republicans be defeated and crushed, we shall rise again. But another nasty compromise, whereby everything is conceded and nothing secured, will so thoroughly disgrace and humiliate us that we can never again raise our heads, and this country becomes a second edition of the Barbary States, as they were sixty years ago. 'Take any form but that.'"

EDITORIAL IN *NEW YORK TRIBUNE*, FEBRUARY 27, 1861

SHALL WE HAVE A FEDERAL UNION?

The border Slave States make certain enormous demands of the American People, as the condition of their future allegiance to the General Government. Many well-meaning, but short-sighted persons clamor for these concessions, in the hope of thereby preserving the Union. They forget that the nature of the concessions demanded, as well as the fact of making them at all, under existing circumstances, will involve the destruction of the Central Power, and must result, if granted, in a dissolution of the Federal Government altogether.

The border Slave States are said to be desirous to maintain the Union. We wish it were so, but unhappily they have, at the outset, assumed a fatal position. They say that the enforcement of the United States laws in any seceding community will be considered "coercion," and that, if it be attempted, they will go with the South. What, then, do they propose to us? A Government which cannot be enforced! Laws which inflict no penalty in case of their violation! But can any human authority be respectable without the means to make itself respected? Can the body politic survive in a state of permanent paralysis?

Now, what are the concessions demanded? The resignation of the very principles and measures on which an overwhelming majority of the People have just instructed the Federal Administration to insist; the establishment of the very policy which the popular verdict has so emphatically condemned; the incorporation into the Constitution of the very Breckinridge Platform which even the corrupt Democratic party was compelled to repudiate!

Suppose we succumb to the will of the minority. Suppose we stifle our convictions, desert our principles, stultify ourselves in our own eyes and in those of our antagonists, and guarantee the perpetuation and extension of Slavery over all present and future territory south of 36° 30'. Suppose, also, that the seceding States are thereby pacified, and induced to resume the outward forms of Union. What then? All this will not preserve nor restore our national unity. On the contrary, it will have destroyed it forever; for we shall have established a new and fatal precedent. Henceforth, the bare majority of any single State can nullify our Government at its pleasure. To-day it is Carolina, to-morrow it may be Rhode Island or Delaware which assumes to dissolve the Confederacy. The will of the majority of the American people constitutionally expressed can no longer decide anything. We have established anarchy and inaugurated chronic civil war. Hereafter, Congress will no longer be a legislature, but a debating society. Its enactments will not be laws, but mere empty expressions of sentiment. The judicial functions of the Supreme Court of the United States will be superseded. The supreme power will be vested solely in the Legislatures of the States, and the forms of national unity will henceforth be an idle mockery. The only real alternative, therefore, is between the enforcement of Federal authority upon every citizen of the United States who resists it, or an actual dissolution of the Federal Government.

If, in our effort to enforce the Federal laws, we find it necessary, or expedient, to slough off the fifteen Slave States, we shall at least have left us a

From Howard Cecil Perkins, ed., *Northern Editorials on Secession*, vol. 1 (New York: D. Appleton-Century Company, 1942), 287–288.

Federal Union of nineteen homogeneous States, free, populous and powerful, with an efficient central organization and a continent for its development. The Southern Confederacy, on the contrary, vitiated by the suicidal principle of State Secession, will be only an aggregated disintegration, a rope of sand, a tossing, incoherent chaos of petty nationalities. There can be no question as to the result. Rent by internal discords and jealousies, the seceding States will, one by one, abolish Slavery and return, under the irresistible force of social gravitation, to the peaceful haven of national unity, under the Constitution handed down to us by our fathers.

The vital question, then, for our consideration is not whether Freedom or Slavery is to be the future guide of the Federal Government, but whether we shall have a Federal Government at all. If so, it must be by prompt, decisive action. We must either treat the fact of Southern Secession as a revolution, and recognize the independence of the seceding States; or we must confront it as treason, and put it down by the military forces of the loyal States. Either course will be frank, honorable and comprehensible. Either mode of action will result in a permanent Federal nationality. Any other proceedings involve a logical fallacy, and must result in imbecility and failure. Shall we maintain a national existence? Shall we have a Federal Union?

EDITORIAL IN *NEW YORK TRIBUNE,* MARCH 27, 1861

THE POLICY OF FORBEARANCE

The Slaveholders' Rebellion is to be successfully met in but one these three ways:

1. By prompt, resolute, unflinching resistance—by the use of force to repel force, whenever the laws are resisted and the authority of the Government defied; or

2. By complete acquiescence in the Secession proclaimed by the insurgents, and the recognition of the revolted States as absolutely independent of the Federal Union; or

3. By a Fabian policy, which concedes nothing, yet employs no force in support of resisted Federal authority, hoping to wear out the insurgent spirit and in due time reestablish the authority of the Union throughout the revolted or seceded States, by virtue of the returning sanity and loyalty of their own people.

We do not assume that this last is the wisest policy, nor yet that it has been resolved on by the new Administration; we propose simply to set forth the grounds on which it is commended and justified.

This Government, it is said, is based not on force but on reason; not on bayonets and battalions, but on good will and general consent. [We wish they would preach this to the Nullifiers, who do not seem to have yet caught the idea.] To war on the Seceders is to give to their yet vapory institutions the strong cement of blood—is to baptize their nationality in the mingled life-blood of friends and foes. But let them severely alone—allow them to wear out the military ardor of their adherents in fruitless drillings and marches, and to exhaust the patience of their fellow-citizens by the amount and frequency of their pecuniary exactions—and the fabric of their power will melt away like fog in the beams of morning sun. Only give them rope, and they will speedily fulfil their destiny—the People, even of South Carolina, rejecting their sway as intolerable, and returning to the mild and paternal guardianship of the Union.

In behalf of this policy, it is urged that the Secessionists are a minority even in the seceded States; that they have grasped power by usurpation and retain it by terrorism; that they never dare submit the question of Union or Disunion fairly and squarely to the people, and always shun a popular vote when they can. In view of these facts, the Unionists of the South urge that the Government shall carry forbearance to the utmost, in the hope that the Nullifiers will soon be overwhelmed by the public sentiment of their own section, and driven with ignominy from power.

And here let us say that, if the Southern Unionists would but themselves evince that courage and outspoken decision which they desire the Federal Government to suppress or conceal, they would have a far stronger claim to be heeded. If they would but fight the battle of the Union unflinchingly, there would be no need of any extraordinary exertion of authority on the part of the Federal power. Had the Unionists of Louisiana saved the Mint, the Sub-Treasury, and the Arsenal, from spoliation, they might have reasonably counseled forbearance on the part of the Federal authorities. But will it do to concede to the Nullifiers a monopoly of the use of force and the manifestation of energy?

"God is patient, because eternal," said Augustine. The law of gravitation can afford to bear and forbear with all seeming counteractions: it is very apt to have its way in the end. The union of the North-West with the South-West is so strongly grounded in physical necessities that it is very hard to persuade the former that the Federal Union is or will be broken up. Meantime, the exactions of the Seceders are so preposterous, that their project of a reconstruction on the basis of a concession of universal and impregnable property in slaves—that is, of slaveholding protected by law in every part of the Union—is so flagrantly at war with the spirit of our age—that the North has not realized that they are in earnest. Yet they are in earnest; and a majority of the loyal subjects of Jeff Davis believe that the North is ready to make its submission, and ask the privilege of adopting the Southern Constitution and suing for admission into the Cotton Republic! For that enormous delusion, the policy of forbearance seems to proffer no immediate cure. We must hesitate before giving our assent to it.

DRAWING CONCLUSIONS:

1. What was Greeley's initial reaction to secession sentiment in the South? How did his views change as this sentiment grew and resulted in the actual secession of southern states?

2. What do Greeley's evolving views on secession suggest about the reactions of northern Republicans to the growing secessionist sentiment in the South?

6.3 LETTERS FROM ABRAHAM LINCOLN TO REPUBLICAN LEADERS

Between the November 1860 election and his inauguration as president the following March, Abraham Lincoln took an active role in crafting the Republican response to secession. Between the election and Inauguration Day, many in Congress worked to find a political compromise that might reverse the growing secessionist sentiment in the South. Lincoln's letters reveal his opposition to any concessions on the issue of slavery extension, which had been the most divisive sectional issue in the years leading up to secession. More importantly, the letters provide clues as to the *reasons* for Lincoln's resistance to compromise on this issue. As you read the letters, think about why Lincoln took such a firm line on the issue of slavery extension. Does he, for instance, seem to think that the alternative to compromise is war? The first two letters are to Republican members of Congress, William Kellogg of Illinois and James T. Hale of Pennsylvania. The final letter is to William H. Seward of New York, among the most influential of Republican politicians and Lincoln's choice to serve as his Secretary of State.

GUIDING QUESTIONS:

1. What reasons does Lincoln give his fellow Republican leaders for taking a hard line on the slavery extension issue?
2. What does Lincoln warn will happen if the Republicans make concessions on the slavery extension issue?
3. What discussion, if any, is there of the potential for war in these letters?

LINCOLN TO WILLIAM KELLOGG

Private & confidential. Hon. William Kellogg. Springfield, Ill. Dec. 11. 1860

My dear Sir—Entertain no proposition for a compromise in regard to the extension of slavery. The instant you do, they have us under again; all our labor is lost, and sooner or later must be done over. Douglas is sure to be again trying to bring in his "Pop. Sov." Have none of it. The tug has to come & better now than later.

You know I think the fugitive slave clause of the constitution ought to be enforced—to put it on the mildest form, ought not to be resisted. In haste Yours as ever A. LINCOLN

LINCOLN TO JAMES T. HALE

Confidential. Hon. J. T. Hale Springfield, Ill. Jan'y. 11th 1861.

My dear Sir—Yours of the 6th is received. I answer it only because I fear you would misconstrue my silence. What is our present condition? We have just carried an election on principles fairly stated to the people. Now we are told in advance, the government

From Roy P. Basler, ed., *The Collected Works of Abraham Lincoln*, Vol. 4 (New Brunswick: Rutgers University Press, 1953), 150.
From Roy P. Basler, ed., *The Collected Works of Abraham Lincoln*, Vol. 4 (New Brunswick: Rutgers University Press, 1953), 172.

shall be broken up, unless we surrender to those we have beaten, before we take the offices. In this they are either attempting to play upon us, or they are in dead earnest. Either way, if we surrender, it is the end of us, and of the government. They will repeat the experiment upon us ad libitum. A year will not pass, till we shall have to take Cuba as a condition upon which they will stay in the Union. They now have the Constitution, under which we have lived over seventy years, and acts of Congress of their own framing, with no prospect of their being changed; and they can never have a more shallow pretext for breaking up the government, or extorting a compromise, than now. There is, in my judgment, but one compromise which would really settle the slavery question, and that would be a prohibition against acquiring any more territory. Yours very truly, A. LINCOLN.

LINCOLN TO WILLIAM H. SEWARD

Private & confidential. Hon. W. H. Seward Springfield, Ills. Feb. 1. 1861

My dear Sir On the 21st. ult. Hon. W. Kellogg, a Republican M.C of this state whom you probably know, was here, in a good deal of anxiety, seeking to ascertain to what extent I would be consenting for our friends to go in the way of compromise on the now vexed question. While he was with me I received a dispatch from Senator Trumbull, at Washington, alluding to the same question, and telling me to await letters. I thereupon told Mr. Kellogg that when I should receive these letters, posting me as to the state of affairs at Washington, I would write you, requesting you to let him see my letter. To my surprise when the letters mentioned by Judge Trumbull came, they made no allusion to the "vexed question." This baffled me so much that I was near not writing you at all, in compliance with what I had said to Judge Kellogg.

I say now, however, as I have all the while said, that on the territorial question—that is, the question of extending slavery under the national auspices,—I am inflexible. I am for no compromise which assists or permits the extension of the institution on soil owned by the nation. And any trick by which the nation is to acquire territory, and then allow some local authority to spread slavery over it, is as obnoxious as any other.

I take it that to effect some such result as this, and to put us again on the high-road to a slave empire is the object of all these proposed compromises. I am against it.

As to fugitive slaves, District of Columbia, slave trade among the slave states, and whatever springs of necessity from the fact that the institution is amongst us, I care but little, so that what is done be comely, and not altogether outrageous. Nor do I care much about New-Mexico, if further extension were hedged against. Yours very truly A. LINCOLN—

DRAWING CONCLUSION:

1. What do these letters reveal about Lincoln's reasons for rejecting compromise on the slavery extension issue during the secession crisis?

From Roy P. Basler, ed., *The Collected Works of Abraham Lincoln*, Vol. 4 (New Brunswick: Rutgers University Press, 1953), 183.

6.4 ABRAHAM LINCOLN TO ALEXANDER STEPHENS, DECEMBER 22, 1860

Abraham Lincoln and Alexander Stephens of Georgia had served together as members of the United States Congress, and they had become friends and political allies. Following Lincoln's election, Stephens was one of the leading opponents of secession in the South. (After Georgia declared independence, Stephens declared his loyalty to his state and was elected vice president of the Confederacy.) In December of 1860, as Georgians debated the secession issue, Lincoln wrote a brief letter to his friend Alexander Stephens. In this letter, Lincoln attempts to provide certain reassurances to southern slave owners. The letter can serve as an example of Lincoln's strategy for dealing with southerners during the secession crisis.

GUIDING QUESTIONS:

1. What is the main point of Lincoln's letter to Stephens? What assurances is he trying to provide southern slave owners?
2. What do you think is Lincoln's motive for sending this letter? Why did he send this letter to Stephens?

LINCOLN TO ALEXANDER H. STEPHENS

For your own eye only. Hon. A. H. Stephens—Springfield, Ill. Dec. 22, 1860

My dear Sir

Your obliging answer to my short note is just received, and for which please accept my thanks. I fully appreciate the present peril the country is in, and the weight of responsibility on me.

Do the people of the South really entertain fears that a Republican administration would, directly, or indirectly, interfere with their slaves, or with them, about their slaves? If they do, I wish to assure you, as once a friend, and still, I hope, not an enemy, that there is no cause for such fears.

The South would be in no more danger in this respect, than it was in the days of Washington. I suppose, however, this does not meet the case. You think slavery is right and ought to be extended; while we think it is wrong and ought to be restricted. That I suppose is the rub. It certainly is the only substantial difference between us. Yours very truly A. LINCOLN

DRAWING CONCLUSION:

1. What does Lincoln's letter to Stephens reveal about Lincoln's response to secession? What is his strategy for dealing with secessionist sentiment in the South?

From Roy P. Basler, ed., *The Collected Works of Abraham Lincoln*, Vol. 4 (New Brunswick: Rutgers University Press, 1953), 160.

6.5 ABRAHAM LINCOLN, FIRST INAUGURAL ADDRESS, MARCH 4, 1861

When Abraham Lincoln took office as President on March 4, 1861, seven southern states had seceded from the union, and representatives from these states had founded the Confederate States of America. Armed conflict between the Confederacy and the United States government had not yet commenced, however. Lincoln's inaugural address, delivered on the day he took office, represents his clearest public statement on the issue of secession. In the speech, Lincoln presents his stance on the slavery issues that had prompted secession as well as on the issue of secession itself.

GUIDING QUESTIONS:

1. What position does Lincoln take in his inaugural address on the slavery extension issue?
2. What position does Lincoln take in his inaugural address on the fugitive slave issue?
3. What position does Lincoln take in his inaugural address on the issue of secession?
4. Under what circumstances, in his inaugural address, does Lincoln say he will employ force against supporters of the Confederacy?

FIRST INAUGURAL ADDRESS—FINAL TEXT

March 4, 1861

Fellow citizens of the United States:

In compliance with a custom as old as the government itself, I appear before you to address you briefly, and to take, in your presence, the oath prescribed by the Constitution of the United States, to be taken by the President "before he enters on the execution of his office."

I do not consider it necessary, at present, for me to discuss those matters of administration about which there is no special anxiety, or excitement.

Apprehension seems to exist among the people of the Southern States, that by the accession of a Republican Administration, their property, and their peace, and personal security, are to be endangered. There has never been any reasonable cause for such apprehension. Indeed, the most ample evidence to the contrary has all the while existed, and been open to their inspection. It is found in nearly all the published speeches of him who now addresses you.

I do but quote from one of those speeches when I declare that "I have no purpose, directly or indirectly, to interfere with the institution of slavery in the States where it exists. I believe I have no lawful right to do so, and I have no inclination to do so." Those who nominated and elected me did so with full knowledge that I had made this, and many similar declarations, and had never recanted them. And more than this, they placed in the platform, for my acceptance, and as a law to themselves, and to me, the clear and emphatic resolution which I now read:

"Resolved, That the maintenance inviolate of the rights of the States, and especially the right of each State to order and control its own domestic institutions according to its own judgment exclusively, is essential to that balance of power on which the perfection and endurance of our political fabric depend;

From Roy P. Basler, ed., *The Collected Works of Abraham Lincoln*, Vol. 4 (New Brunswick: Rutgers University Press, 1953), 262–271.

and we denounce the lawless invasion by armed force of the soil of any State or Territory, no matter under what pretext, as among the gravest of crimes."

I now reiterate these sentiments: and in doing so, I only press upon the public attention the most conclusive evidence of which the case is susceptible, that the property, peace and security of no section are to be in anywise endangered by the now incoming Administration. I add too, that all the protection which, consistently with the Constitution and the laws, can be given, will be cheerfully given to all the States when lawfully demanded, for whatever cause—as cheerfully to one section, as to another.

There is much controversy about the delivering up of fugitives from service or labor. The clause I now read is as plainly written in the Constitution as any other of its provisions:

"No person held to service or labor in one State, under the laws thereof, escaping into another, shall, in consequence of any law or regulation therein, be discharged from such service or labor, but shall be delivered up on claim of the party to whom such service or labor may be due."

It is scarcely questioned that this provision was intended by those who made it, for the reclaiming of what we call fugitive slaves; and the intention of the law-giver is the law. All members of Congress swear their support to the whole Constitution—to this provision as much as to any other. To the proposition, then, that slaves whose cases come within the terms of this clause, "shall be delivered up," their oaths are unanimous. Now, if they would make the effort in good temper, could they not, with nearly equal unanimity, frame and pass a law, by means of which to keep good that unanimous oath?

There is some difference of opinion whether this clause should be enforced by national or by state authority; but surely that difference is not a very material one. If the slave is to be surrendered, it can be of but little consequence to him, or to others, by which authority it is done. And should any one, in any case, be content that his oath shall go unkept, on a merely unsubstantial controversy as to how it shall be kept?

Again, in any law upon this subject, ought not all the safeguards of liberty known in civilized and humane jurisprudence to be introduced, so that a free man be not, in any case, surrendered as a slave? And might it not be well, at the same time, to provide by law for the enforcement of that clause in the Constitution which guarranties that "The citizens of each State shall be entitled to all previleges and immunities of citizens in the several States?"

I take the official oath to-day, with no mental reservations, and with no purpose to construe the Constitution or laws, by any hypercritical rules. And while I do not choose now to specify particular acts of Congress as proper to be enforced, I do suggest, that it will be much safer for all, both in official and private stations, to conform to, and abide by, all those acts which stand unrepealed, than to violate any of them, trusting to find impunity in having them held to be unconstitutional.

It is seventy-two years since the first inauguration of a President under our national Constitution. During that period fifteen different and greatly distinguished citizens, have, in succession, administered the executive branch of the government. They have conducted it through many perils; and, generally, with great success. Yet, with all this scope for precedent, I now enter upon the same task for the brief constitutional term of four years, under great and peculiar difficulty. A disruption of the Federal Union heretofore only menaced, is now formidably attempted.

I hold, that in contemplation of universal law, and of the Constitution, the Union of these States is perpetual. Perpetuity is implied, if not expressed, in the fundamental law of all national governments. It is safe to assert that no government proper, ever had a provision in its organic law for its own termination. Continue to execute all the express provisions of our national Constitution, and the Union will endure forever—it being impossible to destroy it, except by some action not provided for in the instrument itself.

Again, if the United States be not a government proper, but an association of States in the nature of contract merely, can it, as a contract, be peaceably unmade, by less than all the parties who made it? One party to a contract may violate it—break it, so to speak; but does it not require all to lawfully rescind it?

Descending from these general principles, we find the proposition that, in legal contemplation, the Union is perpetual, confirmed by the history of the Union itself. The Union is much older than the Constitution. It was formed in fact, by the Articles of Association in 1774. It was matured and continued by the Declaration of Independence in 1776. It was further matured and the faith of all the then thirteen States expressly plighted and engaged that it should be perpetual, by the Articles of Confederation in 1778. And finally, in 1787, one of the declared objects for ordaining and establishing the Constitution, was "to form a more perfect union."

But if destruction of the Union, by one, or by a part only, of the States, be lawfully possible, the Union is less perfect than before the Constitution, having lost the vital element of perpetuity.

It follows from these views that no State, upon its own mere motion, can lawfully get out of the Union,—that resolves and ordinances to that effect are legally void; and that acts of violence, within any State or States, against the authority of the United States, are insurrectionary or revolutionary, according to circumstances.

I therefore consider that, in view of the Constitution and the laws, the Union is unbroken; and, to the extent of my ability, I shall take care, as the Constitution itself expressly enjoins upon me, that the laws of the Union be faithfully executed in all the States. Doing this I deem to be only a simple duty on my part; and I shall perform it, so far as practicable, unless my rightful masters, the American people, shall withhold the requisite means, or, in some authoritative manner, direct the contrary. I trust this will not be regarded as a menace, but only as the declared purpose of the Union that it will constitutionally defend, and maintain itself.

In doing this there needs to be no bloodshed or violence; and there shall be none, unless it be forced upon the national authority. The power they confided to me, will be used to hold, occupy, and possess the property, and places belonging to the government, and to collect the duties and imposts; but beyond what may be necessary for these objects, there will be no invasion—no using of force against, or among the people anywhere. Where hostility to the United States, in any interior locality, shall be so great and so universal, as to prevent competent resident citizens from holding the Federal offices, there will be

no attempt to force obnoxious strangers among the people for that object. While the strict legal right may exist in the government to enforce the exercise of these offices, the attempt to do so would be so irritating, and so nearly impracticable with all, that I deem it better to forego, for the time, the uses of such offices.

The mails, unless repelled, will continue to be furnished in all parts of the Union. So far as possible, the people everywhere shall have that sense of perfect security which is most favorable to calm thought and reflection. The course here indicated will be followed, unless current events, and experience, shall show a modification, or change, to be proper; and in every case and exigency, my best discretion will be exercised, according to circumstances actually existing, and with a view and a hope of a peaceful solution of the national troubles, and the restoration of fraternal sympathies and affections.

That there are persons in one section, or another who seek to destroy the Union at all events, and are glad of any pretext to do it, I will neither affirm or deny; but if there be such, I need address no word to them. To those, however, who really love the Union, may I not speak?

Before entering upon so grave a matter as the destruction of our national fabric, with all its benefits, its memories, and its hopes, would it not be wise to ascertain precisely why we do it? Will you hazard so desperate a step, while there is any possibility that any portion of the ills you fly from, have no real existence? Will you, while the certain ills you fly to, are greater than all the real ones you fly from? Will you risk the commission of so fearful a mistake?

All profess to be content in the Union, if all constitutional rights can be maintained. Is it true, then, that any right, plainly written in the Constitution, has been denied? I think not. Happily the human mind is so constituted, that no party can reach to the audacity of doing this. Think, if you can, of a single instance in which a plainly written provision of the Constitution has ever been denied. If, by the mere force of numbers, a majority should deprive a minority of any clearly written constitutional right, it might, in a moral point of view, justify revolution—certainly would, if such right were a vital one. But such is not our case. All the vital rights of minorities, and of individuals, are so plainly assured to them, by affirmations and negations, guarranties and prohibitions, in the Constitution, that controversies never arise concerning them. But no organic law can ever be framed with a provision specifically applicable to every question which may occur in practical administration. No foresight can anticipate, nor any document of reasonable length contain express provisions for all possible questions. Shall fugitives from labor be surrendered by national or by State authority? The Constitution does not expressly say. May Congress prohibit slavery in the territories? The Constitution does not expressly say. Must Congress protect slavery in the territories? The Constitution does not expressly say.

From questions of this class spring all our constitutional controversies, and we divide upon them into majorities and minorities. If the minority will not acquiesce, the majority must, or the government must cease. There is no other alternative; for continuing the government, is acquiescence on one side or the other. If a minority, in such case, will secede rather than acquiesce, they make a precedent which, in turn, will divide and ruin them; for a minority of their own will secede from them, whenever a majority refuses to be controlled by such minority. For instance, why may not any portion of a new confederacy, a year or two hence, arbitrarily secede again, precisely as portions of the present Union now claim to secede from it. All who cherish disunion sentiments, are now being educated to the exact temper of doing this. Is there such perfect identity of interests among the States to compose a new Union, as to produce harmony only, and prevent renewed secession?

Plainly, the central idea of secession, is the essence of anarchy. A majority, held in restraint by constitutional checks, and limitations, and always changing easily, with deliberate changes of popular opinions and sentiments, is the only true sovereign of a free people. Whoever rejects it, does, of necessity, fly to anarchy or to despotism. Unanimity is impossible; the rule of a minority, as a permanent arrangement, is wholly inadmissable; so that, rejecting the majority principle, anarchy, or despotism in some form, is all that is left.

I do not forget the position assumed by some, that constitutional questions are to be decided by the Supreme Court; nor do I deny that such decisions must be binding in any case, upon the parties to a suit, as to the object of that suit, while they are also entitled to very high respect and consideration, in all paralel cases, by all other departments of the government. And while it is obviously possible that such decision may be erroneous in any given case, still the evil effect following it, being limited to that particular case, with the chance that it may be over-ruled, and never become a precedent for other cases, can better be borne than could the evils of a different practice. At the same time the candid citizen must confess that if the policy of the government, upon vital questions, affecting the whole people, is to be irrevocably fixed by decisions of the Supreme Court, the instant they are made, in ordinary litigation between parties, in personal actions, the people will have ceased, to be their own rulers, having, to that extent, practically resigned their government, into the hands of that eminent tribunal. Nor is there, in this view, any assault upon the court, or the judges. It is a duty, from which they may not shrink, to decide cases properly brought before them; and it is no fault of theirs, if others seek to turn their decisions to political purposes.

One section of our country believes slavery is right, and ought to be extended, while the other believes it is wrong, and ought not to be extended. This is the only substantial dispute. The fugitive slave clause of the Constitution, and the law for the suppression of the foreign slave trade, are each as well enforced, perhaps, as any law can ever be in a community where the moral sense of the people imperfectly supports the law itself. The great body of the people abide by the dry legal obligation in both cases, and a few break over in each. This, I think, cannot be perfectly cured; and it would be worse in both cases after the separation of the sections, than before. The foreign slave trade, now imperfectly suppressed, would be ultimately revived without restriction, in one section; while fugitive slaves, now only partially surrendered, would not be surrendered at all, by the other.

Physically speaking, we cannot separate. We cannot remove our respective sections from each other, nor build an impassable wall between them. A husband

and wife may be divorced, and go out of the presence, and beyond the reach of each other; but the different parts of our country cannot do this. They cannot but remain face to face; and intercourse, either amicable or hostile, must continue between them. Is it possible then to make that intercourse more advantageous, or more satisfactory, after separation than before? Can aliens make treaties easier than friends can make laws? Can treaties be more faithfully enforced between aliens, than laws can among friends? Suppose you go to war, you cannot fight always; and when, after much loss on both sides, and no gain on either, you cease fighting, the identical old questions, as to terms of intercourse, are again upon you.

This country, with its institutions, belongs to the people who inhabit it. Whenever they shall grow weary of the existing government, they can exercise their constitutional right of amending it, or their revolutionary right to dismember, or overthrow it. I can not be ignorant of the fact that many worthy, and patriotic citizens are desirous of having the national constitution amended. While I make no recommendation of amendments, I fully recognize the rightful authority of the people over the whole subject, to be exercised in either of the modes prescribed in the instrument itself; and I should, under existing circumstances, favor, rather than oppose, a fair opportunity being afforded the people to act upon it.

I will venture to add that, to me, the convention mode seems preferable, in that it allows amendments to originate with the people themselves, instead of only permitting them to take, or reject, propositions, originated by others, not especially chosen for the purpose, and which might not be precisely such, as they would wish to either accept or refuse. I understand a proposed amendment to the Constitution—which amendment, however, I have not seen, has passed Congress, to the effect that the federal government, shall never interfere with the domestic institutions of the States, including that of persons held to service. To avoid misconstruction of what I have said, I depart from my purpose not to speak of particular amendments, so far as to say that, holding such a provision to now be implied constitutional law, I have no objection to its being made express, and irrevocable.

The Chief Magistrate derives all his authority from the people, and they have conferred none upon him to fix terms for the separation of the States. The people themselves can do this also if they choose; but the executive, as such, has nothing to do with it. His duty is to administer the present government, as it came to his hands, and to transmit it, unimpaired by him, to his successor.

Why should there not be a patient confidence in the ultimate justice of the people? Is there any better, or equal hope, in the world? In our present differences, is either party without faith of being in the right? If the Almighty Ruler of nations, with his eternal truth and justice, be on your side of the North, or on yours of the South, that truth, and that justice, will surely prevail, by the judgment of this great tribunal, the American people.

By the frame of the government under which we live, this same people have wisely given their public servants but little power for mischief; and have, with equal wisdom, provided for the return of that little to their own hands at very short intervals.

While the people retain their virtue, and vigilence, no administration, by any extreme of wickedness or folly, can very seriously injure the government, in the short space of four years.

My countrymen, one and all, think calmly and well, upon this whole subject. Nothing valuable can be lost by taking time. If there be an object to hurry any of you, in hot haste, to a step which you would never take deliberately, that object will be frustrated by taking time; but no good object can be frustrated by it. Such of you as are now dissatisfied, still have the old Constitution unimpaired, and, on the sensitive point, the laws of your own framing under it; while the new administration will have no immediate power, if it would, to change either. If it were admitted that you who are dissatisfied, hold the right side in the dispute, there still is no single good reason for precipitate action. Intelligence, patriotism, Christianity, and a firm reliance on Him, who has never yet forsaken this favored land, are still competent to adjust, in the best way, all our present difficulty.

In your hands, my dissatisfied fellow countrymen, and not in mine, is the momentous issue of civil war. The government will not assail you. You can have no conflict, without being yourselves the aggressors. You have no oath registered in Heaven to destroy the government, while I shall have the most solemn one to "preserve, protect and defend" it.

I am loath to close. We are not enemies, but friends. We must not be enemies. Though passion may have strained, it must not break our bonds of affection. The mystic chords of memory, stretching from every battlefield, and patriot grave, to every living heart and hearthstone, all over this broad land, will yet swell the chorus of the Union, when again touched, as surely they will be, by the better angels of our nature.

DRAWING CONCLUSIONS:

1. What does the inaugural address reveal about Lincoln's strategy for resolving the secession crisis?

2. What does the inaugural address reveal about the issues over which Lincoln is prepared to go to war? What issues is he not willing to go to war over?

6.6 ABRAHAM LINCOLN, PROCLAMATION CALLING MILITIA AND CONVENING CONGRESS, APRIL 15, 1861

In his inaugural address, President Lincoln stated that, while he would not initiate conflict, he would defend federal military installations within the Confederate states. One such installation was Fort Sumter, a federal outpost in the harbor of Charleston, South Carolina. On April 11, 1861, Confederate forces demanded the surrender of the fort. Under orders from Lincoln, the federal commander at Fort Sumter refused to submit. On the morning of April 12, Confederate forces launched an artillery assault on the fort. Two days later, the federal garrison surrendered. On April 15, the President issued a proclamation calling for the states to provide 75,000 militia soldiers to suppress the rebellion. (At the time, the United States had a very small standing army. To suppress the rebellion, Lincoln would need a substantial number of short-term volunteer troops.) This proclamation can be considered Lincoln's declaration of war against the Confederacy and those who supported it. Response to Lincoln's proclamation across the North was enthusiastic. The slave states of Virginia, North Carolina, Tennessee, and Arkansas, however, refused to provide troops and instead seceded from the Union and joined the Confederacy, bringing the total number of Confederate states to eleven.

GUIDING QUESTION:

1. What reasons does Lincoln give in his proclamation for requesting that the states provide troops?

PROCLAMATION CALLING MILITIA AND CONVENING CONGRESS

April 15, 1861
By the President of the United States
A Proclamation.

Whereas the laws of the United States have been for some time past, and now are opposed, and the execution thereof obstructed, in the States of South Carolina, Georgia, Alabama, Florida, Mississippi, Louisiana and Texas, by combinations too powerful to be suppressed by the ordinary course of judicial proceedings, or by the powers vested in the Marshals by law,

Now therefore, I, Abraham Lincoln, President of the United States, in virtue of the power in me vested by the Constitution, and the laws, have thought fit to

call forth, and hereby do call forth, the militia of the several States of the Union, to the aggregate number of seventy-five thousand, in order to suppress said combinations, and to cause the laws to be duly executed. The details, for this object, will be immediately communicated to the State authorities through the War Department.

I appeal to all loyal citizens to favor, facilitate and aid this effort to maintain the honor, the integrity, and the existence of our National Union, and the perpetuity of popular government; and to redress wrongs already long enough endured.

I deem it proper to say that the first service assigned to the forces hereby called forth will probably be to repossess the forts, places, and property which have been seized from the Union; and in every event, the utmost

From Roy P. Basler, ed., *The Collected Works of Abraham Lincoln*, Vol. 4 (New Brunswick: Rutgers University Press, 1953), 331–332.

care will be observed, consistently with the objects aforesaid, to avoid any devastation, any destruction of, or interference with, property, or any disturbance of peaceful citizens in any part of the country.

And I hereby command the persons composing the combinations aforesaid to disperse, and retire peaceably to their respective abodes within twenty days from this date.

Deeming that the present condition of public affairs presents an extraordinary occasion, I do hereby, in virtue of the power in me vested by the constitution, convene both Houses of Congress. Senators and Representatives are therefore summoned to assemble at their respective chambers, at 12 o'clock, noon, on Thursday, the fourth day of July, next, then and there to consider and determine, such measures, as, in their wisdom, the public safety, and interest may seem to demand.

In Witness Whereof I have hereunto set my hand, and caused the Seal of the United States to be affixed.

Done at the city of Washington this fifteenth day of April in the year of our Lord One thousand, Eight hundred and Sixty-one, and of the Independence of the United States the Eighty-fifth.

ABRAHAM LINCOLN

DRAWING CONCLUSION:

1. What does this proclamation reveal about the reasons that Lincoln went to war against the Confederacy and its supporters?

ADDITIONAL RESOURCES

Barney, William L. *The Road to Secession: A New Perspective on the Old South.* New York: Praeger Publishers, 1972.

Boritt, Gabor, ed. *Why the Civil War Came.* New York: Oxford University Press, 1996.

Crofts, Daniel W. *Lincoln and the Politics of Slavery: The Other Thirteenth Amendment and the Struggle to Save the Union.* Chapel Hill: University of North Carolina Press, 2016.

Dew, Charles B. *Apostles of Disunion: Southern Secession Commissioners and the Causes of the Civil War.* Charlottesville: University of Virginia Press, 2001.

Fehrenbacher, Don E. *Sectional Crisis and Southern Constitutionalism.* Baton Rouge: Louisiana State University Press, 1995.

Gienapp, William E. *The Origins of the Republican Party, 1852–1856.* New York: Oxford University Press, 1987.

Holt, Michael F. *The Political Crisis of the 1850s.* New York: John Wiley & Sons, 1978.

McPherson, James M. "Antebellum Southern Exceptionalism: A New Look at an Old Question." *Civil War History* 29 (September 1983): 230–244.

Oakes, James. *The Scorpion's Sting: Antislavery and the Coming of the Civil War.* New York: W.W. Norton and Company, 2014.

Pessen, Edward. "How Different from Each Other Were the Antebellum North and South?" *American Historical Review* 85 (December 1980): 1119–1149.

Potter, David M. *The Impending Crisis, 1848–1861.* New York: Harper Row, 1976.

Potter, David M. *The South and the Sectional Conflict.* Baton Rouge: Louisiana State University Press, 1968.

Stampp, Kenneth M. *And the War Came: The North and the Secession Crisis, 1860–61.* Baton Rouge: Louisiana State University Press, 1950.

Thomas, Emory M. *The Dogs of War, 1861.* New York: Oxford University Press, 2011.

INDEX

Note: In this index, the following symbols are used: *italicized* numbers for maps, and *T* for the Timeline located before the main text.

A

abolitionism/abolitionists
    "Appeal of the Independent Democrats in Congress," 37–41
    emergence, 34
    Frederick Douglass on slavery, 34–37
    Georgia secessionists and, 82–83, 91, 98
    Mississippi secessionists and, 77
    New Orleans secessionists and, 69
    right of slave property, 77
    sectional conflict, 5–6
    southern opposition, 44, 56
    Sumner, 50, 58–59
anti-abolitionist violence, 5
Articles of Confederation, 114

B

Beale, Howard K., 4
Border Ruffians, 58, 59
border slave states, 95, 106
Boston, 17–18
Brazil, 27
Brooks, Preston, 50
    Northern rebuke, 59, 60–61
    sympathy for, 55, 56–57
Brown, Albert G., 42–43
Brown, Joseph E., public letter, 90–95
Butler, Andrew, 50, 51

C

Charleston, 17
Chase, Salmon P., 37–41
civil war
    beginnings of, 3
    casualties in, 3
    debate over causes, 4
    Lincoln's options, 8–9
    secession, 8
    sectional conflict, 4–8
    timing of, 9–10
Cleveland, Ohio, 51